ANOTHER JESUS?
The Eucharistic Christ
and the
New Evangelization

*To Tori,
Sincerely in Christ,
Roger Oakland
July 24/04.*

by
Roger Oakland

with Jim Tetlow

Another Jesus?
The Eucharistic Christ and the New Evangelization
By Roger Oakland, with Jim Tetlow
Published by Understand the Times
P.O. Box 27239
Santa Ana, CA 92799

Copyright 2004 Understand the Times

ISBN 0- 9700609-7-1

Library of Congress Control Number 2004090454

Edited by Susan Moore

Unless otherwise indicated, all Scripture quotations in this book have been taken from the New King James Version of the Bible, copyright 1979, 1980, 1982, by Thomas Nelson Publishers. Used by permission.

Table of Contents

Chapter Twelve —

Acknowledgment

Another Jesus? The Eucharistic Christ and the New Evangelization, could not have been written without a team effort.

Chapter 4 and chapter 10 were written by Jim Tetlow. These two chapters are adapted from appendix A and B in his book *Messages from Heaven.* As well, Jim spent countless hours reading through the original manuscript providing key suggestions and additions. The appendix of this book was co-authored with Jim. Without his diligent assistance and valuable knowledge as a former Roman Catholic, this book would not have been possible.

Second, I would also like to thank Susan Moore for the role she played in editing. Third, a special thanks to Brad Myers for assisting in research and documentation. Fourth, thanks to John Shaffer for the cover design and the helpful insights he provided. Finally, thanks to Sascha and Marion Svoboda for their assistance in getting this book published.

Introduction

The apostle Paul was a man with a passion for the truth. While his ministry was clearly focused on proclaiming the saving grace of the gospel of Jesus Christ, he was also concerned when he saw the truth being compromised by Satan's subtle deceptive plan.

While Paul had made every effort to teach the church at Corinth the truth about Jesus and the fact that He had died upon the cross to save them from their sins, false teachers and false teaching had infiltrated the church. Obviously some were being led astray. For this reason he expressed his concerns the following way:

> But I fear, lest somehow, as the serpent deceived Eve by his craftiness, so your minds may be corrupted from the simplicity that is in Christ. For if he who comes preaches another Jesus whom we have not preached, or if you receive a different spirit which you have not received, or a different gospel which you have not accepted—you may well put up with it! [1]

The title for the book you are holding in your hand is inspired by this portion of Scripture. The urgent message that Paul was warning the Corinthians about is the same message I believe God wants proclaimed today.

---

[1] 2 Corinthians 11:3-4

Satan's plan to deceive Eve, and the Corinthian church, has not been altered throughout the ages. The fact that there is "another gospel" inspired by "another spirit" that seduces people into believing they know Jesus Christ when in reality they do not, is not new. Current trends seem to indicate we may be headed down a similar pathway leading toward a strong deception that has the potential of deceiving the whole world.

It is for this reason that I have written this book. There are two major objectives. First, it is to be a wakeup call to all those who know the Jesus of the Bible so that they heed the call to contend for the faith and warn others. Second, it is a warning to all who may think they know Jesus Christ but instead are deceived into believing in "another" Jesus. Jesus made it clear there are serious consequences for those who think they have believed in Him, but instead have been deceived by an experiential form of Christianity centered on the miraculous instead of an understanding of the gospel.

Proclaiming these thoughts in a message referred to as "The Sermon on the Mount" recorded in the Book of Matthew, Jesus said:

> Not everyone who says to Me, "Lord, Lord," shall enter the kingdom of heaven, but he who does the will of My Father in heaven. Many will say to Me in that day, "Lord, Lord, have we not prophesied in Your name, cast out demons in Your name, and done many wonders in Your name?" And then I will declare to them, "I never knew you; depart from Me, you who practice lawlessness!" [2]

---

[2] Matthew 7:21-23

These sobering words should be a reminder to all those who profess the name of Jesus to pay close attention to the statement Jesus made. Imagine what it would be like to be a sincere Jesus follower, then find out you were not following Jesus. While it is possible to encounter miraculous experiences in the name of Jesus, it is not these experiences that qualify anyone to go to heaven. Instead one could spend eternity in hell.

The facts that you will read about in *Another Jesus?* fell into place over a period of several years. As each piece of a jigsaw puzzle adds to the overall completeness of a picture, current events coupled with insights from the Bible compelled me to write this. While it would be easier not to face the opposition the message contained within this book will bring, I am reminded from Scripture, contending for a faith based on God's Word is not an option. As Jude wrote:

> Beloved, while I was very diligent to write to you concerning our common salvation, I found it necessary to write to you exhorting you to contend earnestly for the faith which was once for all delivered to the saints. For certain men have crept in unnoticed, who long ago were marked out for this condemnation, ungodly men, who turn the grace of our God into lewdness and deny the only Lord God and our Lord Jesus Christ. [3]

It should be obvious from the title and the illustration observed on the front cover, my objective in writing this book will be to confront one of the major foundational beliefs promoted by the Catholic Church — the idea of transubstantiation, the concept that Christ actually manifests

---

[3] Jude 3-4

on the altar and is contained in a monstrance (container), when a priest "consecrates" a wafer.

While this books deals with a sacred foundational Catholic belief, it is not my objective to attack or offend Catholics. I have written this book because I have a love and a compassion for those who have been deceived. The subject of where human souls spend eternity is a serious matter. The Bible teaches that deception is authored by Satan. The devil's goal is to destroy mankind and take as many lost souls hostage with him to hell as he can. His ultimate plan is to deceive as many people as possible in the name of the Savior, Jesus Christ. I am convinced when we see people being deceived in this manner, we must warn them in love.

The Bible clearly teaches that the end times will be characterized by a strong spiritual delusion that blinds many from the true gospel and also leads those who have believed into apostasy. While the deception covers a vast spectrum of satanic doctrines, this book will be focused on one particular aspect — false appearances of Jesus. As Jesus warned:

> Then if anyone says to you, "Look, here is the Christ!" or "There!" do not believe it. For false christs and false prophets will rise and show great signs and wonders to deceive, if possible, even the elect. See, I have told you beforehand. [4]

I challenge everyone who reads this book, to do so with an open mind. First, consider carefully and honestly what God has revealed in His Word. Second, consider the facts

---

[4] Matthew 24:24-25

that are presented in light of current trends. May the light of God's Word shine bright and reveal the truth.

Chapter One
Deception in His Name

The Bible teaches that God has an adversary. Since the fall of Adam and Eve in the Garden of Eden, the world has been influenced by Satan, the one who "deceives the whole world." [1]

His goal has always been to blind human minds "lest the light of the gospel of the glory of Christ, who is the image of God, should shine on them." [2] Yet, when a person heeds the light of God's word, his heart and mind is illuminated to the truth.

The Scriptures also reveal that Satan's agenda to deceive mankind will intensify just before Jesus returns. Satan will employ a final effort to deceive the world, this time in the name of the Savior, Jesus Christ. This chapter will document this scenario showing that the Bible forewarns us about this time of strong spiritual delusion.

The Invisible War

Are you aware that we are in the midst of warfare that takes place all around us, twenty-four hours a day, every day of the week? This battle does not involve the use of

---

[1] Revelation 12:9
[2] 2 Corinthians 4:4

physical artillery. This battle takes place in the spiritual dimension.

Just as a bullet, a grenade or a bomb can bring about death and destruction, the missiles fired at us by our spiritual opponents are equally devastating. Only in this case, the human mind is the battleground. The information we input into our minds can be spiritually lethal.

Paul the Apostle made this point clear. Writing to the Ephesians, he warned them about the unseen dimension that endeavors to attack human beings and destroy them spiritually:

> Put on the whole armor of God, that you may be able to stand against the wiles of the devil. For we do not wrestle against flesh and blood, but against principalities, against powers, against the rulers of the darkness of this age, against spiritual hosts of wickedness in the heavenly places. [3]

After identifying the enemy, Paul outlined the strategy that is necessary if we are going to understand how the enemy works and how we should react. He stated:

> Therefore take up the whole armor of God, that you may be able to withstand in the evil day, and having done all, to stand. Stand therefore, having girded your waist with truth, having put on the breastplate of righteousness, and having shod your feet with the preparation of the gospel of peace; above all, taking the shield of faith with which you will be able to quench all the fiery darts of the wicked one. [4]

---

[3] Ephesians 6:11-13
[4] Ephesians 6:13-16

The "truth" or "shield of faith" that Paul was writing about is the Word of God. Jesus also made this very clear. "Thy Word is truth," He proclaimed. [5]

It is vitally important then, if we are going to protect ourselves from Satan's "fiery darts" to do so knowing all that God has said, as recorded in the Bible.

A More Sure Word

Another important principle found in the Bible is the fact that we can know the future with complete confidence before it happens — that is of course, when the Bible makes reference to the future. As Peter wrote:

> And so we have the prophetic word confirmed, which you do well to heed as a light that shines in a dark place, until the day dawns and the morning star rises in your hearts; knowing this first, that no prophecy of Scripture is of any private interpretation, for prophecy never came by the will of man, but holy men of God spoke as they were moved by the Holy Spirit. [6]

Bible statements with regard to the future are God-inspired and accurate. It is also apparent there are certain events or circumstances that God wants us to know about in advance. Peter tells us that it is important that we pay careful attention when God reveals the future to us. These accurate statements will be like a light shining in a dark place, that help us to understand and be prepared.

Counterfeit Christs

The twenty-fourth chapter of Matthew is one of the most well-known and studied portions of Scripture when

---

[5] John 17:17
[6] 2 Peter 1:19-20

it comes to learning about end-times events. This chapter records numerous statements by Jesus who was responding to the question asked by His disciples: "Tell us, when will these things be? And what will be the sign of Your coming, and of the end of the age?" [7]

While Jesus' response to this question shed light upon a number of events that would occur, there is one area that He warned about that clearly appears to be the most significant sign of all that were listed. While earthquakes, famines, wars, pestilence, and lawlessness would be on the upswing, even more important than these things He highlighted spiritual deception as the major sign to watch out for. This spiritual deception, He proclaimed, would occur in His name.

For example, consider His first response to the question:

> Take heed that no one deceives you. For many will come in My name, saying, "I am the Christ," and will deceive many. [8]

It is obvious these words of Jesus were spoken in a way that commands our attention. There is a sense of urgency and a call to awareness — *take heed* means to beware or to be alert. The fact the deception would take place in the name of Christ and that "many" would be deceived by "many" is also significant. While this statement alone should be sufficient to warn us about a last days spiritual deception, Jesus further emphasized the magnitude of this deception by saying: "Then many false prophets will rise up and deceive many." [9]

---

[7] Matthew 24:3
[8] Matthew 24:3-4
[9] Matthew 24:11

Jesus continued to describe various other events that would happen before His coming, and then He returned to the topic of deception that would occur in His name. This time, Jesus was even more specific regarding what form this deception would take. He warned about a time when there would be false appearances of beings proclaiming to be "Christ," and these appearances would be accompanied by what He described as "great signs and wonders" that were of the deceptive variety. We read:

> Then if anyone says to you, "Look, here is the Christ!" or "There!" do not believe it. For false christs and false prophets will rise and show great signs and wonders to deceive, if possible, even the elect. [10]

Furthermore, adding clarity to the nature of these false appearances, Jesus stated:

> Therefore if they say to you, "Look, He is in the desert!" do not go out; or "Look, He is in the inner rooms!" do not believe it. For as the lightning comes from the east and flashes to the west, so also will the coming of the Son of Man be. [11]

Secret Chambers

As we read through Matthew 24, it is apparent that the spiritual deception that takes place in the name of Jesus is associated with false appearances. But even more specifically, Jesus wanted us to know the exact locations where these false appearances would be occurring.

In order that there would be no need to speculate regarding this important matter, Jesus provided exact locations where these false appearances would occur. While

---

[10] Matthew 24:23-24
[11] Matthew 24:26-27

our English translations say that counterfeit christs would appear in the "secret chambers" [12] or "inner rooms" [13] or "inner chambers," [14] a look at the original Greek word *tameion* provides some very interesting insight. With reference to *Strong's Concordance*, the actual meaning of the Greek word *tameion* that is translated as *inner rooms* is:

> tameion (tam-i'-on); neuter contraction of a presumed derivative of tamias (a dispenser or distributor; akin to temno, to cut); a dispensary or magazine, i.e. a chamber on the ground-floor or interior of an Oriental house (generally used for storage or privacy, a spot for retirement) [15]

In other words, the original Greek word *tameion*, actually refers to some kind of storage container or dispensary. A vessel or a container to store or dispense a counterfeit christ? That sounds strange, but as you continue to read, is it possible that this future prediction of Christ is in the process of being fulfilled today?

He Told Us Beforehand

The twenty-fifth verse of Matthew chapter 24 is a statement made by Jesus that has profound importance: "See, I have told you beforehand." The disciples had asked for signs of the times that would be apparent at the end of the age. Jesus answered their question. By answering the disciples' question, Jesus is enabling anyone who reads

---

[12] King James Version
[13] New King James Version
[14] American Standard Version
[15] Biblesoft's New Exhaustive Strong's Numbers and Concordance with Expanded Greek-Hebrew Dictionary, 1994, Biblesoft and International Bible Translators, Inc.

these verses today to also know beforehand. We have been warned ahead of time so that when we see these things that were foretold, we will know that we are living at the period of time proceeding the soon return of Jesus.

Another Jesus?

The title of this book did not come about without serious thought and consideration. It should be apparent that *Another Jesus?* was chosen to stimulate all professing Christians to search out the Scriptures carefully and honestly with regard to the identity of the true Jesus. Is there a difference between the Eucharistic Christ of Roman Catholicism and the Jesus of the Bible? This is the question that is being asked.

The Bible teaches our eternal destiny depends on knowing the true Jesus — who He is and what He has done. If one of Satan's goals is to deceive people into believing in "another Jesus" then all who call themselves Christians need to be on guard. In order to know Jesus, we need to be certain who He is. As Jesus stated in John chapter 8:

> Therefore I said to you that you will die in your sins; for if you do not believe that I am He, you will die in your sins. [16]

The only way we can be certain that we know the biblical Jesus is to know the Word of God. As Jesus Himself stated:

> Abide in Me, and I in you. As the branch cannot bear fruit of itself, unless it abides in the vine, neither can you, unless you abide in Me. I am the vine, you are the branches. He who abides in Me, and I in him, bears much fruit; for without Me you can do nothing. If anyone does not abide in Me, he is

---

[16] John 8:24

cast out as a branch and is withered; and they gather them and throw them into the fire, and they are burned. If you abide in Me, and **My words abide in you**, you will ask what you desire, and it shall be done for you. [17]

In spite of these clear warnings, we know the Scriptures tell us that many will be deceived into believing in "another Jesus". These people were convinced they knew the biblical Jesus but instead had been seduced by Satan. In Jesus' own words:

Not everyone who says to Me, "Lord, Lord," shall enter the kingdom of heaven, but he who does the will of My Father in heaven. Many will say to Me in that day, "Lord, Lord, have we not prophesied in Your name, cast out demons in Your name, and done many wonders in Your name?" And then I will declare to them, **"I never knew you..."** [18]

The very fact that Jesus never knew "them" means they never knew Him. This clearly suggests that sincere "Jesus" believing people can be deceived and spend eternity in hell because they chose to believe in "another Jesus."

I am aware that some who read the title of this book may be offended. Some may make the following comment: *"Another Jesus? The Eucharistic Christ and the New Evangelization* makes the claim that the Jesus Christ of Roman Catholicism is not the Jesus of the Bible—how absurd and blasphemous. Everyone knows that Catholics believe in an orthodox biblical historical Jesus, born of a virgin in Bethlehem, the Son of God, the Jesus who died on a cross and was raised from the dead. How can anyone dare suggest this is not the true Jesus who can save us from our sins?"

---

[17] John 15:4-7
[18] Matthew 7:21-23

However, as this book will document, there are significant differences. The apostle Paul warned about "another Jesus." [19] Do you suppose this "other Jesus" he was warning about was similar to Jesus or very different? If Satan wanted to counterfeit the Jesus of the Bible, wouldn't it be reasonable to suggest this counterfeit Jesus would be a biblical Jesus mixed together with a few characteristics that were not biblical?

Consider why Paul warned the Galatians and the Corinthians about this very danger. They had embraced the biblical Jesus, but with a twist. They had accepted the biblical Jesus but added on an additional requirement for salvation. Instead of Jesus alone it was Jesus plus works.

Paul did not hesitate to speak the truth with boldness. His rebuke was harsh:

> O foolish Galatians! Who has bewitched you that you should not obey the truth, before whose eyes Jesus Christ was clearly portrayed among you as crucified? [20]

It is important therefore that we be armed with a scriptural arsenal to help us identify how to discern imposters that masquerade in Jesus' name. In Second Corinthians chapter 11, the fourth verse, Paul gave us the only answer we need to detect a counterfeit. He said: "For if he who comes preaches another Jesus whom **we have not preached...**" Any Jesus that is not the Jesus according to Scripture is not the Jesus of Scripture.

Catholics are Required to Embrace the Eucharist

It is true that many Catholics do not accept Rome's doctrines concerning transubstantiation. Many Roman

---

[19] 2 Corinthians 11:4
[20] Galatians 3:1

Catholics deny that Jesus Christ is literally and physically present in the Eucharist. However, the Church's position on this is clear. Anyone who denies any aspect of the Church's teachings on the Eucharist is to be "anathema"! The following quotes taken directly from *The Canons and Decrees of The Council of Trent* and referenced in *The Catechism of the Catholic Church* are very clear:

> If anyone denies that in the sacrament of the most Holy Eucharist are contained truly, really and substantially the body and blood together with the soul and divinity of our Lord Jesus Christ, and consequently the whole Christ, but says that He is in it only as in a sign, or figure or force, let him be anathema. [21]

> If anyone says that Christ received in the Eucharist is received spiritually only and not also sacramentally and really, let him be anathema. [22]

> If anyone says that in the holy sacrament of the Eucharist, Christ, the only begotten Son of God, is not to be adored with the worship of *latria*; also outwardly manifested, and is consequently neither to be venerated with a special festive solemnity, nor to be solemnly borne about in procession according to the laudable and universal rite and custom of holy Church, or is not to be set publicly before the people to be adored and that the adorers thereof are idolaters, let him be anathema. [23]

---

[21] H. J. Schroeder, O.F., *The Canons and Decrees of The Council of Trent*, Rockford, IL, Tan Books and Publishers, Inc., 1978, page 79, Canon 1.
[22] Ibid., page 80, Canon 8.
[23] Ibid., Canon 6.

The End Times Christ

While I have written other books on the topic of end-times spiritual deception, this book will focus very specifically on the "false appearances of counterfeit christs" as warned by Jesus. More specifically, this book will lay out a scenario, documented by facts, based on current events that are associated with a "Christ" that is supposedly appearing on altars in Catholic churches all over the world. I am referring to the Eucharistic Jesus that supposedly manifests by a supernatural process called transubstantiation, based on the belief that a Catholic priest has the power to transform a wafer into the actual presence of Jesus. It is this "Eucharistic Christ" that can be contained in a tabernacle or monstrance [24] and even put on display for adoration.

It is obvious from Jesus' words of warning that the deception He was referring to would be very effective and convincing. Many would be deceived by these false appearances and the miracles that would be associated with them.

The scenario that I am about to present based on current events has the potential to line up exactly with what Jesus said would happen. If this is so, then it is absolutely imperative to warn people what is happening and where we are headed.

---

[24] A monstrance is a special container that houses the consecrated Communion wafer. See chapter 5.

Chapter Two
A Missionary Vision

Over the past several years, a number of facts have been brought to my attention resulting in the documentation for this book. Every book that I have written that has dealt with the topic of spiritual deception has come together in a similar way. First, I notice a particular topic or subject matter that is brought to my attention from several different sources. Second, a number of Scriptures come to mind that shed light on the topic. Third, I am challenged with the seriousness of the subject matter. Later I am compelled with a sense of urgency to share a warning to others. Fourth, more articles, books, photographs and information continue to fall into place adding further support and documentation.

The book you are reading is no exception. The journey began in the late 1990s when the word *Eucharist* [1] caught my attention from a number of sources. As I was not familiar with this term, it was necessary for me to do further research.

I discovered that the Roman Catholic Church's doctrine of the Eucharist was based on the concept of transubstan-

---

[1] The Eucharist is known by several names including, the Blessed Sacrament or Communion Host.

tiation, a belief that the Catholic priest has the power to turn a wafer of bread into the actual body, blood, soul and divinity of Jesus. Further, I learned that this basic belief was the very foundation of the Catholic faith.

But there was another aspect of the Eucharist that became apparent to me. I came across a number of testimonies given by individuals who had encountered what they described as a Eucharistic experience. This life-changing event, they claimed, had been influential in their conversion to the Roman Catholic Church.

Thus, I was very interested when I came across a press release from the Vatican regarding statements made by Pope John Paul II about the significance of the Eucharist, and calling for the Eucharist to be the center of the missionary vision for the Catholic Church. The pope had made these statements at a Eucharistic Congress held in Rome during the year of Catholic Jubilee in June of 2000.

The Pope and Missions

In his homily, presented at the 47th International Eucharistic Congress, June 21, 2000, Pope John Paul II spoke of the Eucharist as the source and focus of the Catholic Church's missionary task. In his own words:

> The Congress puts the Eucharist at the center of the Great Jubilee of the Incarnation and expresses all its spiritual, ecclesial and missionary depth. It is from the Eucharist, in fact, that the Church and every believer draw the indispensable strength to proclaim and bear witness before all to the Gospel of salvation. The celebration of the Eucharist, the sacrament of the Lord's Passover, *is in itself a mis-*

sionary event, which plants the fertile seed of new life in the world. [2]

Further elaborating on what the pope described as the missionary aspect of the Eucharist, his message continued:

The Eucharist is a "missionary" sacrament not only because the grace of missions flows from it, but also because it contains in itself the principle and eternal source of salvation for all. [3]

This call to a missionary vision centered on the Eucharist fascinated me. The pope, the head of the Catholic Church, was calling upon Catholics to become missions oriented by focusing their attention on the importance of the Eucharist. The importance of this was further reflected in the following passionate statement:

This reflection on the meaning and missionary content of the Eucharist cannot fail to mention those outstanding *"missionaries"* and witnesses to the faith and love of Christ who are *the martyrs.* The relics of the martyrs, preserved since antiquity ... are a clear sign of the power flowing from Christ's sacrifice. This spiritual energy spurs all who are nourished by the Body of the Lord to offer their lives for him and for their brothers and sisters by giving themselves without reserve and, if necessary, even by shedding their blood. [4]

---

[2] "Holy Father's Homily for Corpus Christi: The Living Father Comes Down from Heaven — Eucharist Spurs Christians to mission," *L'Osservatore Romano,* June 28, 2000, cited July 3, 2000, Online posting: www.vatican.va/news_services/or/or_eng/text.html #4 [italics in the original.]

[3] Ibid.

[4] Ibid.

Finally, in an effort to encourage Catholics to become involved in a program to promote Eucharistic evangelization, the pope challenged his followers by stating:

> May the International Eucharistic Congress, through the intercession of Mary, Mother of the Christ offered in sacrifice for us, help to make believers more conscious of the missionary responsibility that stems from their participation in the Eucharist. The "Body given" and the "Blood poured out" are the highest criterion they must always use in giving themselves for the world's salvation. [5]

The Knights of Columbus

In February of 2002, I noticed an advertisement in the *Orange County Register* that also drew my attention to the Eucharist. This advertisement, placed in the paper by the Knights of Columbus, seemed to confirm that Pope John Paul's vision for Eucharistic evangelization was underway.

At the top of the full-page advertisement there was a photo of the pope handing a wafer to a nun during Mass. These words were written beneath:

> God wants to share His life with us by uniting us to His Son, Jesus Christ—not only mentally or spiritually but completely. This is why Jesus gave us the Holy Eucharist, His own Body and Blood to eat. Holy Communion is food for the whole believer, heart and mind, body and soul. And the food is Je-

---

[5] Ibid.

sus Himself. It is Christ's Body and Blood: not just a symbol, but the real thing. [6]

Beneath this paragraph there was an offer made by the Knights of Columbus to provide further information to all who were interested in knowing more about the Eucharist. The advertisement continued:

> We invite you to send for our free booklet on the Holy Eucharist, to find out what Catholics believe and why. We don't call or put you on a mailing list: we just want you to find out about the gift Christ wants to give. Find out the truth about the Holy Eucharist, and find the secret of the saints. [7]

As I was interested in knowing more about what Catholics believe, in particular about the Eucharist, I clipped out the coupon that was offered as part of the advertisement and sent it to the Knights of Columbus address. Several weeks later I received a booklet in the mail titled "Questions and Answers on the Eucharist." The booklet, described as part of "The Veritas Series" also had an additional subtitle on the first page — "Proclaiming the Faith in the Third Millennium." [8]

I immediately read through the booklet. Now my understanding of the Eucharist and its significance to the Catholic Church with regard to the pope's call to evangeli-

---

[6] *Parade Magazine*, insert placed in *Orange County Register*, February 17, 2002, page 7.

[7] Ibid.

[8] "Questions and Answers on the Eucharist: Proclaiming the Faith in the Third Millennium," Pennsylvania Catholic Conference, 2000, Harrisburg, PA, General Editor Father John A. Farren, O.P., Director of the Catholic Information Service Knights of Columbus Supreme Council.

zation became somewhat clearer. Under a subheading "Why is the Eucharist So Important to the Church," I read:

> The Eucharist is the heart of the Church's life. In the celebration of the mystery of faith, Christ himself is present to his people. Rich in symbolism and richer in reality, the Eucharist bears within itself the whole reality of Christ and mediates his saving work to us. In short, when the Church gathers in worship of God, and offers the Eucharistic sacrifice, not only is Christ really and truly present under the appearances of bread and wine, but he also continues his saving work of salvation. [9]

There were other statements that caught my attention. From a section titled "What Is Meant By Christ's Real Presence in the Eucharist?" I read:

> The way in which Jesus is present in the Eucharist cannot be explained in physical terms because it transcends the ordinary necessities of space and measurement. It is a supernatural mystery that the person who becomes fully present at Mass is the same Risen Savior who is seated at the right hand of the Father. In becoming present sacramentally, Christ's condition does not change. He does not have to leave heaven to become present on earth.

In another section titled "What Is Meant By Transubstantiation?" I gathered further insight:

> ...that by the consecration of bread and wine there takes place a change in the whole substance of the bread into the substance of the body of Christ our Lord and the whole substance of the wine into the substance of his blood. This change the holy

---

[9] Ibid., page 4.

Catholic Church has fittingly and properly called transubstantiation. [10]

But my introduction to the Eucharist and my understanding of its significance to the Catholic faith was still not complete. There was another area of paramount importance that opened my understanding and provided one of the major insights that has inspired this book. In another section of the Knights of Columbus booklet called "Why Is The Eucharist Kept In The Tabernacle?" I read:

> The real presence endures after the celebration of the Eucharistic liturgy. It is for this reason there is a tabernacle in churches. Once communion has been distributed, the remaining hosts are placed in the tabernacle to provide viaticum for those who turn to the Church in the final hour and also to provide a focal point for prayer and worship of Christ and his real presence. [11]

Now, for the first time, I had been made aware of the idea that the Catholic Church teaches that "the real presence of Christ" is actually contained and resides in a tabernacle within every Catholic church. The tabernacle chamber contains the Eucharist and is positioned inside every Catholic church on the altar. According to Webster's Dictionary, the Eucharistic tabernacle is "a receptacle for the consecrated elements of the Eucharist; *esp*: an ornamental locked box used for reserving the Communion Hosts." Throughout the world Catholics are encouraged to visit, pray to, worship and adore "Christ" who is stored inside these tabernacles. An additional statement made this even clearer:

---

[10] Ibid., page 11.
[11] Ibid.

With the passage of time, reverent reflection led the Church to enrich Eucharistic devotion. Faith that Jesus is truly present in the sacrament led believers to worship Christ dwelling with us permanently in the sacrament. Wherever the sacrament is, there is Christ who is our Lord and our God; hence he is ever to be worshipped in this mystery. Such worship is expressed in many ways: genuflection, in adoration of the Eucharist and in the many forms of Eucharistic devotion that faith has nourished. [12]

Eucharistic Evangelization

But there was more. The Knights of Columbus booklet also emphasized "Eucharistic evangelization," exactly what the pope had called for at the Eucharistic Congress in June of 2000. At the conclusion of the booklet, there was a clarion call for Catholics to better understand what the Church taught so they would be better Catholics. In a section called "Why Is It Important To Prepare Myself To Receive The Eucharist?" the following statement was made:

> Recent polls indicate that a significant number of Catholics do not have a complete understanding of the Eucharist and specifically the real presence of Christ in the Blessed Sacrament. Whatever the cause of such misunderstanding of the faith, all who approach the table of the Lord need to recognize the significance of their action and the importance of their spiritual preparation. [13]

Following this statement, another clearly worded paragraph, reveals the true significance of the Blessed Sacrament as the heart and core of the Roman Catholic faith. In order to be a "Christian" according to the Roman Catholic

---

[12] Ibid., page 12.
[13] Ibid., page 13.

tradition, transubstantiation must be embraced without exception. We read:

> Often at weddings, funerals and other religious oc-
> casions where those who do not share our faith are
> present, there is the temptation among those pres-
> ent to try to avoid any type of awkwardness by in-
> viting non-Catholics to receive the Eucharist. Those
> who are not in full communion with the Church,
> however, are not permitted to participate at the ta-
> ble of the Lord as if they were full members, shar-
> ers of the full sacramental life of the Church.
> Reception of communion creates the public per-
> ception that the one receiving the Lord is in full
> unity with the Catholic Church. [14]

And finally, if there still is any doubt with regard to the importance of the Eucharist as the focal point of evangeli-zation and the very heart of the Catholic belief system, consider the following statement taken from the Knights of Columbus booklet:

> Catholics believe that the Eucharist is an action of
> celebrating community signifying oneness in faith,
> life and worship of the community. Reception of
> the Eucharist by Christians not fully united with us
> would imply a oneness which does not yet exist
> and for which we must all pray. [15]

Father Tom Forest on Evangelization

The pope's declaration at the Eucharistic Congress in June of 2000 and the Knights of Columbus booklet pro-moting the Eucharist as the heart of what Catholics mean by evangelization, reminded me of a statement made by

---

[14] Ibid., page 13-14.
[15] Ibid., page 14.

Father Tom Forest in 1990. I had come across this quote while doing research for my book, *New Wine and the Babylonian Vine.*

During the late 1990s, while Evangelical Protestants and Catholics were making progress joining hands and disregarding differences ("Evangelicals and Catholics Together"), I discovered there was strong evidence of an underlying Catholic agenda to entice all those who were not Catholic to become Catholic.

For example, at a gathering of Evangelicals and Catholics at an Indianapolis conference in 1990, Father Tom Forest spoke to a group that was exclusively Catholic. During this meeting he went on record by stating:

> Our job is to make people as richly and as fully Christian as we can make them by bringing them into the Catholic Church. So evangelization is never fully successful, it's only partial, until the convert is made a member of Christ's body by being led into the [Catholic] church.

> No, you don't just invite someone to become a Christian. You invite them to become Catholics... Why would this be so important? First of all, there are seven sacraments, and the Catholic Church has all seven. On our altars we have the body of Christ; we drink the blood of Christ. Jesus is alive on our altars...We become one with Christ in the Eucharist...

> As Catholics we have Mary, and that Mom of ours, Queen of Paradise, is praying for us till she sees us in glory. As Catholics we have the papacy, a history of popes from Peter to John Paul II...we have the rock upon which Christ did build His Church. Now as Catholics — now I love this one — we have purgatory. Thank God! I'm one of those people

who would never get to the Beatific Vision without it. It's the only way to go....

So as Catholics...our job is to use the remaining decade evangelizing everyone we can in the Catholic Church, into the body of Christ and into the third millennium of Catholic history. [16]

Connecting the Dots

It was obvious to me that the missionary vision centered around a focus on the Eucharist was a topic worthy of research. If the pope and others were emphasizing the importance of the Eucharist for evangelization and there was evidence that conversions were happening because of Eucharistic experiences, this subject obviously demanded further attention.

As more and more information fell into place, verses from the Bible shed light on the trend that was unfolding. Eventually I put an outline together and presented the topic *Another Jesus? The Eucharistic Christ and the New Evangelization* to several small groups. A number of people encouraged me to share the information in the form of a book. This book is the result.

---

[16] "Roman Catholic Doubletalk at Indianapolis '90," *Foundation*, July-August 1990, excerpts from talk by Fr. Tom Forest to the Roman Catholic Saturday morning training session.

Chapter Three
Understanding the Eucharist

The title of this book contains the word *Eucharist*. Like me, you may have heard the word but if asked to explain the meaning you would have difficulty doing so.

In the previous chapter we introduced the subject of the Eucharist by quoting the pope and also by examining several statements taken from a Knights of Columbus booklet that was designed to help people understand the true meaning and significance of the Eucharist. However, when dealing with this topic and the importance of this idea in relation to the subject matter of this book, there are other aspects of the Eucharist that need to be added.

The purpose of this chapter will be to examine the Eucharist in more detail by examining various Catholic sources.

Transubstantiation

It is not possible to comprehend the meaning of the Eucharist without having an understanding of the term *transubstantiation*. Catholic author Joan Carol Cruz provides the following definition:

The word officially approved by the Council of
Trent to express the changing of the entire sub-
stance of bread and wine into the Body and Blood
of Christ. After the Consecration only the appearances or "accidents" (color, taste, smell, quantity,
etc.) of bread and wine remain. [1]

According to this view, during the act of consecration
(performed by a priest), the bread (wafer) and wine miraculously are transformed into the actual presence of Jesus Christ. While the bread and wine may appear to be
still bread and wine following the consecration, a mystical
process has occurred, it is believed. Thus Jesus is supposed
to be physically present on the altar and physically eaten
when the recipient ingests the consecrated wafer.

To further verify that this view is the basis of Roman
Catholic doctrine, I will quote from the January/February
2000 issue of *Envoy Magazine*, a bimonthly journal of
Catholic apologetics and evangelization. The purpose for
publishing this magazine "is to present the truths of the
Catholic Faith in a fresh, contemporary style, featuring today's top Catholic writers, full color-graphics and upbeat
innovative format." [2] According to the magazine's mission
statement "*Envoy Magazine* is a division of the Missionaries
of Faith Foundation, a non-profit organization dedicated
to spreading the gospel through the broadcast and print
media, personal   evangelization   and Bible study programs. [3]

---

[1] Joan Carol Cruz, *Eucharistic Miracles*, Tan Books and Publishers, Rockford, IL, 1987, page xiii, Imprimatur, Phillip M. Hannan, Archbishop of New Orleans, April 25, 1986, p. xxii.
[2] *Envoy Magazine*, January/February 2000, Envoy Communications, Granville, OH, page 2.
[3] Ibid.

Located on the front cover of the January/February 2000 issue, is an illustration that graphically shows the hands of a Catholic priest holding up a "consecrated wafer," the sky and clouds are background. The title on the magazine cover reads: "This Looks Like Bread, Tastes Like Bread, and Feels Like Bread. Is this God?" The word "God?" is in large print. The "O" (which is actually the consecrated wafer) is the conspicuous object on the cover.

An article by author Dave Armstrong, with the same title as the one illustrated on the front cover is found on page 34 of the magazine. The following statement made by Armstrong will further document the Catholic view of transubstantiation. Armstrong states:

> In conclusion, let's take a look at the actual nature of what occurs in the miracle of transubstantiation. *Accidental* change occurs when non-essential outward properties (accidents) are changed in some fashion. For example, water can take on the properties of solidarity as ice, and of vapor as steam, all the while remaining chemically the same. *Substantial* change, on the other hand, produces something entirely different. In our every day *natural* experience, a change of substance is always accompanied by a corresponding change of accidents, or outward properties. One example would be the metabolizing of food, which literally changes to become part of our bodies as a result of digestion.

> But the Eucharist is a *supernatural* transformation, in which substantial change occurs *without* accidental change. Thus the outward properties of bread and wine continue after consecration, but their essence and *substance* are replaced by the sub-

stance of the true and actual Body and Blood of Christ. [4]

It is also important to mention that David Armstrong is a convert to Catholicism. He admits that at one time, he did not understand the importance of transubstantiation. However, Armstrong now asks: "How could I have had such an insufficient understanding of the Holy Eucharist: the central focus of Christian worship?" [5]

Like many others who have converted to Catholicism, Armstrong was enlightened to the significance of the Eucharist by studying the "Church Fathers." He writes:

> The evidence of the Real Presence of Christ in the Eucharist, among the Church Fathers, is the most compelling of any historic doctrine which Protestants now dispute. [6]

Now Armstrong is convinced that the consecrated wafer is God and that it represents the true and actual body and blood of Christ. He concludes:

> This is what requires faith, and what causes many to stumble, because it is a miracle of a very sophisticated nature, one that doesn't lend itself to empirical or scientific "proof." But, in a sense, it is no more difficult to believe than the changing of water to ice, in which the outward properties change, while the substance (molecular structure) doesn't. The Eucharist merely involves the opposite scenario: the substance changes while the outward properties don't. [7]

---

[4] Ibid., page 40. [Italics in the original]
[5] Ibid., page 35.
[6] Ibid., page 36.
[7] Ibid., page 40.

The Power of the Priest

According to the Catholic faith, Catholic priests have the power to manifest the presence of Jesus on an altar. At the moment of Consecration, the miraculous process know as transubstantiation supposedly occurs. As Joan Carol Cruz states in her book *Eucharistic Miracles:*

> The wafer of unleavened bread which becomes the Body and Blood of Christ at the moment of Consecration in the Mass. (One large Host for the priest and many small Hosts for the Congregation are consecrated at Mass). The word derives from the Latin *hostia,* or "victim" since in the Holy Sacrifice of the Mass Jesus Christ offers Himself to God the Father as the victim and propitiation for our sins. (Thus each Mass is the renewal of the one Sacrifice of Calvary). [8]

In order to substantiate this view, Catholics claim that transubstantiation was taught by Jesus at the Last Supper. Further, it is also believed it was at this time that Jesus anointed His disciples with this power to transform bread and wine into the actual presence of Christ. In turn, the Catholic Church teaches that this power was then transferred down through the centuries to a select chosen priesthood by apostolic succession and priestly ordination.

David Pearson, another contributing author for *Envoy Magazine,* explains this scenario in his article "Do Catholics Worship Cookies?" He writes:

> ...the first communicants received the First Communion from the Great High Priest himself. The unblemished Lamb of God, about to be sacrificed for their sins and those of the whole world for all

---

[8] Cruz.

time, fed his twelve Apostles — our first band of bishops — His very body and blood, under the appearance of bread and wine, from His own hand.

That's what happens today in every Mass. Jesus, God's perfect Passover lamb, uses the graces of apostolic succession and priestly ordination (the "laying on of hands" in the early Church) to feed every generation on His flesh and blood until He returns in glory.

When Jesus comes again at the end of time, He will not have a single drop more glory than He has right now upon the altars and in the tabernacles of our churches," writes Catholic theologian Scott Hahn in *The Lamb's Supper: The Mass as Heaven on Earth.*

Today, even though we are thousands of miles from that little hill in Israel, we are there with Jesus in the upper room, and we are there with Jesus in heaven, whenever we go to Mass." And he might have added, wherever we remain — or return — after Mass to adore Jesus in the Blessed Sacrament. [9]

Scott Hahn on the Power of Priests

Dr. Scott Hahn is another converted Catholic and zealous promoter of the Eucharist. Later in this book we will examine his testimony in detail. Both he and his wife Kimberly have testified that the Eucharist played a major role in their conversion to the Catholic Church. Hahn, a theology professor at a Catholic University in Steubenville, Ohio, and author of a number of books, also writes a regular column called "Scripture Matters" for *Envoy Maga-*

---

[9] David Pearson, "Do Catholics Worship Cookies?" *Envoy,* Granville, OH, Volume 7.2, 2003, page 14.

zine. In an article titled "The Paternal Order of Priests: An Open Letter to Our Catholic Clergy, In a Time of Crisis," he enthusiastically reminds Catholic priests of the power they have been endowed with. He writes:

> As priests of the New Covenant, you are conformed to Christ in a unique and powerful way. Christian tradition speaks of ordination in the most astonishing terms. It is a commonplace of Catholic speech to say that the priest is alter Christus, another Christ. The Catechism tells us further that the priest acts "in the person of Christ" and like Christ, he is a "living image of God the Father" (CCCnn. 1548.9). Through the ministry of ordained priests, the presence of Jesus Christ "is made visible in the community of believers." [10]

Then continuing to elevate the priesthood to a level of godhood, Hahn exalts ordinary sinful men, by saying:

> Theologians refer to the ontological change—a change in the man's very being—that occurs with the sacrament of Holy Orders. Ordination "confers an indelible spiritual character" that is permanent and imprinted...for ever" (CCC nn. 1582-3). [11]

Then comparing this supernatural transformation attributed to priesthood with the transformation that occurs during the consecration of the Host, Hahn concludes:

> The great Cappadocian Father Gregory of Nyssa compared this sacramental change to the transubstantiation that occurs in the Eucharist. "The bread," he explains, "is at first common bread. But

---

[10] Scott Hahn, "The Paternal Order of Priests: An Open Letter to Our Catholic Clergy, In a Time of Crisis," insert in *Envoy*, Granville, OH, Volume 7.2, 2003.
[11] Ibid.

when the sacramental action consecrates it, it is called the Body of Christ... The same power of the word makes the priest worthy of veneration and honor. The new blessing separates him from common, ordinary life. Yesterday he was one of the crowd, one of the people. Now, suddenly he has become a guide, a leader, a teacher of righteousness, an instructor of hidden mysteries. And this he does without any change in body and form. But while he appears to be the man he was before, his invisible soul has really been transformed to a higher condition by some invisible power and grace." [12]

Eucharistic Evangelization

In chapter 2, I quoted Father Tom Forest, Director of Evangelization 2000, a Vatican spokesman. He indicated that true evangelization must be based on the fact that Christians are not complete until they become Catholics. He pointed out the importance of the sacraments that lay the foundation for what it means to be Catholic.

Catholic sources state that the sacrament of the Eucharist is the most important sacrament. For example, in *Eucharistic Miracles,* Joan Carol Cruz, writes:

(The Eucharist is) the Sacrament in which, under the appearances of bread and wine, the Body and Blood of Christ are truly, really and substantially present as the grace-producing food of our souls. More specifically, the consecrated Host and the consecrated "wine," that is, the Precious Blood. [13]

Or according to the Catholic Catechism, we read:

---

[12] Ibid.
[13] Cruz.

The Eucharist is "the source and summit of the Christian life." The other sacraments, and indeed all ecclesiastical ministries and works of the apostolate, are bound up with the Eucharist and are oriented toward it. For the blessed Eucharist is contained in the whole spiritual good of the Church, namely Christ himself, our Pasch." [14]

Further, to make it absolutely clear the Eucharist is at the heart and core of what it means to be a Catholic, the Catechism further notes:

In brief, the Eucharist is the sum and summary of our faith: "Our way of thinking is attuned to the Eucharist, and the Eucharist in turn confirms our way of thinking. [15]

It is also fact that the Catholic Church teaches that the Eucharist actually re-presents Christ as a sacrifice for sins and that during the "sacrifice of the Mass" Christ is daily being sacrificed for our sins in an unbloody manner. As stated in the Catholic Catechism:

The sacrifice of Christ and the sacrifice of the Eucharist are *one single sacrifice*: "The victim is one and the same: the same now offers through the ministry of priests, who then offered himself on the cross; only the manner of offering is different." In this divine sacrifice which is celebrated in Mass, the same Christ who offered himself once in a bloody manner on the altar of the cross is contained and is offered in an unbloody manner. [16]

---

[14] *Catechism of the Catholic Church*, An Image Book, Doubleday, New York, 1994, page 334.
[15] Ibid., page 344.
[16] Ibid.

It should be apparent then that the Eucharistic Jesus present on every Catholic altar is of paramount importance to Catholicism and the Catholic faith. Truly the Eucharistic Jesus is the Jesus of Catholicism. However, is the Eucharistic Jesus the Jesus of the Bible?

In the next chapter we will examine the Scriptures with regard to the Catholic teaching on transubstantiation. This chapter, written by Jim Tetlow, and adapted from his previously published book, *Messages From Heaven*, will provide a scriptural basis for the refutation of the idea of transubstantiation.

Chapter Four
The Eucharist:
A Biblical Review

As I mentioned in the introduction, this book has been assembled by gathering information that has fallen into place over several years from a variety of sources. While I have been on this journey I have met others who are also on the same road researching, gathering facts and analyzing them from a biblical perspective. One person who has contributed greatly in my search for the truth is a good friend, Jim Tetlow.

I first met Jim after speaking at a prophecy conference in upstate New York. Jim's goal, as mine, has been to produce sound materials on the topic of biblical apologetics that present Christianity intelligently and understandably. Over the past several years I have had the privilege of working with Jim on three major video projects: *Countdown to Eternity, A Question of Origins,* and *Messages from Heaven.*

Jim has also authored a book titled *Messages from Heaven: A Biblical Examination of the Queen of Heaven's Messages in the End Times,* published by Eternal Productions. The book deals with the topic of Marian apparitions and how they can be interpreted in light of Scripture. Jim was raised Catholic and was taught the fundamental beliefs of the Roman Catholic Church.

Jim has given me permission to include in this book some of the important topics that he had written about in *Messages from Heaven*. The rest of this chapter is an adaptation of appendix B of his book.

The Eucharist Holds Center Stage

The Eucharist is the focus of Roman Catholic faith. It is the central component of the Mass. It is the sacrament of sacraments. Without question, the Church of Rome regards the doctrine of the Eucharist and Christ's real presence to be of utmost importance. Failure to acknowledge this truth is considered grave sacrilege by Rome. The official Catechism of the Catholic Church leaves no doubt on this point.

> The Eucharist is "the source and summit of the Christian life." The other sacraments, and indeed all ecclesiastical ministries and works of the apostolate, are bound up with the Eucharist and oriented toward it. [1]

> The Sunday Eucharist is the foundation and confirmation of all Christian practice. For this reason the faithful are obliged to participate in the Eucharist. [2]

> Sacrilege is a grave sin especially when committed against the Eucharist, for in this sacrament the true

---

[1] *Catechism of The Catholic Church,* An Image Book, published by Doubleday, 1994, para. 1324, page 368.
[2] Ibid., para. 2181, page 583.

Body of Christ is made substantially present for us. [3]

Catholic Doctrine

The Catholic Church teaches that once a Catholic priest has consecrated the wafer of bread during Communion, the wafer turns into the literal and real body, blood, soul, and divinity of Jesus Christ. [4] Therefore, the Communion Host is no longer bread, but Jesus, under the appearance of bread, and is therefore worthy of adoration and worship. The Catholic Catechism states succinctly —

> In the most blessed sacrament of the Eucharist "the body and blood, together with the soul and divinity, of our Lord Jesus Christ and, therefore, the whole Christ is truly, really, and substantially contained." [5]

> The Church and the world have a great need for Eucharistic worship. Jesus awaits us in this sacrament of love. Let us not refuse the time to go to meet him in adoration, in contemplation full of faith, and open to making amends for the serious offenses and crimes of the world. Let our adoration never cease. [6]

> Because Christ himself is present in the sacrament of the altar, he is to be honored with the worship of adoration. [7]

---

[3] Ibid., para. 2120, page 570.
[4] This process is called transubstantiation and is described in the Catechism of the Catholic Church, paragraphs 1373-1377 and 1413, on pages 383-385 and page 395.
[5] Catechism of the Catholic Church, para. 1374, page 383.
[6] Ibid., para. 1380, pages 385, 386.
[7] Ibid., para. 1418, pages 395.

What Does the Bible Teach?

We have documented what the Roman Catholic Church teaches concerning the Eucharist. But what does the Bible teach? The Bible encourages believers to study the "whole counsel" [8] of God's Word and to "test all things; hold fast what is good" (1 Thessalonians 5:21). Every believer is to "be diligent to present yourself approved to God, a worker who does not need to be ashamed, rightly dividing the word of truth" (2 Timothy 2:15). To obey God's command to test all things, we will search the Scriptures to determine what the Bible teaches concerning the Lord's Supper.

The Last Supper was celebrated by first century Christians in obedience to Jesus' words "do this in remembrance of Me" (Luke 22:19). This observance was established by the Lord at the Last Supper when He symbolically offered Himself as the Paschal Lamb of atonement. His actual death the next day fulfilled the prophecy. Only Paul uses the phrase *Lord's Supper* [9] although it is alluded to in Revelation 19:9, where we are told that believers will celebrate the "marriage supper of the Lamb." Church fathers began to call the occasion the *Eucharist* meaning *thanksgiving* from the blessing pronounced over the bread and wine after about A.D. 100. Christians have celebrated the Lord's Supper regularly as a sign of the new covenant sealed by Christ's death and resurrection. [10] Today, the Eucharist means far more than simply thanksgiving.

This is My Body

So what exactly did Jesus ordain during the Last Supper? Here is the Bible's description of the events sur-

---

[8] Acts 20:27
[9] 1 Corinthians 11:20
[10] Holman Bible Dictionary, Parsons Technology, 1994.

rounding the Lord's Supper. At the Last Supper "[Jesus] took bread, gave thanks and broke it, and gave it to them, saying, 'This is My body which is given for you; do this in remembrance of Me.' Likewise He also took the cup after supper, saying, 'This cup is the new covenant in My blood, which is shed for you'" (Luke 22: 19, 20).

Furthermore, proponents of the Catholic Eucharist point to Jesus' words recorded in the sixth chapter of John's Gospel. Though this chapter does not deal with the Last Supper, Jesus' words certainly appear to relate to the Communion meal:

"I am the living bread which came down from heaven. If anyone eats of this bread, he will live forever; and the bread that I shall give is My flesh, which I shall give for the life of the world." The Jews therefore quarreled among themselves, saying, "How can this Man give us His flesh to eat?" Then Jesus said to them, "Most assuredly, I say to you, unless you eat the flesh of the Son of Man and drink His blood, you have no life in you. Whoever eats My flesh and drinks My blood has eternal life, and I will raise him up at the last day. For My flesh is food indeed, and My blood is drink indeed." (John 6:51-55).

We will now examine the Word of God to understand the context and meaning of the Scriptures that pertain to Communion. [11]

---

[11] Scriptural instructions concerning Communion can be found in the following verses: Matthew 26:17-35; Mark 14:12-31; Luke 22:7-23; John 13:1-17, 26 and 1 Corinthians 11:17-34.

Metaphors and Similes

Throughout the Bible, context determines meaning. Bible-believing Christians know to take the Bible literally unless the context demands a figurative or symbolic interpretation. Before exploring Jesus' words in John chapter 6 and elsewhere, let's review a few examples of symbolism in the Scriptures. All scholars would agree that the following verses are metaphorical. An explanation follows each verse.

Oh, taste and see that the LORD is good (Psalm 34:8).

(Try and experience God's promises to find if they are true.)

"Whoever drinks of the water that I shall give him will never thirst. But the water that I shall give him will become in him a fountain of water springing up into everlasting life" (John 4:14).

(For those who receive the gift of salvation, Christ's Spirit shall dwell in their souls assuring them of everlasting life.)

Moreover He said to me, "Son of man, eat what you find; eat this scroll, and go, speak to the house of Israel." So I opened my mouth, and He caused me to eat that scroll (Ezekiel 3:1, 2).

(Receive into your heart, internalize, and obey God's Word.)

At one point Jesus said, "Destroy this temple, and in three days I will raise it up." [12] The Jews thought He spoke of the literal temple in Jerusalem, but if we keep reading

---

[12] John 2:19

we find that Jesus was referring to His body. [13] On another occasion, Jesus said, "I am the true vine." [14] Of course we know that Jesus did not mean that He was a literal grape vine twisting around a post. When the Bible says God hides us under His wings, [15] we know that God is not a bird with feathers. God is the source of all life and our provider and protector, and these figures vividly illustrate this.

Throughout the Bible, figurative language is used to compare one thing to another so that the listeners can easily visualize and understand. It is apparent from searching the entire council of God that the Lord often uses metaphors to paint images for the reader. In fact the Bible tells us that Jesus regularly used parables to figuratively describe one thing as something else. [16] Jesus Himself stated, "These things I have spoken to you in figurative language..." (John 16:25). However, the Bible should always be interpreted literally unless the context demands a symbolic explanation. So what does the context of John's Gospel and the other Gospels demand?

John Chapter 6

If we read the entire sixth chapter of John's Gospel, we not only get the context, but also some startling insights into what Jesus meant when He said we must eat His flesh and drink His blood. John chapter 6, begins with the account of Jesus feeding five thousand, followed by the account of Jesus walking on water. Starting in verse 22, we find that on the following day, people were seeking Jesus for the wrong reasons, which we understand from Jesus'

---

[13] John 2:20-21
[14] John 15:1
[15] Psalm 91:4
[16] Matthew 13:34

words in verses 26 and 27: "You seek Me, not because you saw the signs, but because you ate of the loaves and were filled. Do not labor for food which perishes, but for food which endures to everlasting life."

These verses begin to frame the context of the verses that follow, specifically, that Jesus emphasized the need for them to seek eternal life. Jesus goes on to explain to them how to obtain eternal life. And in verse 28, when the people ask Jesus "What shall we do, that we may work the works of God?" Jesus replies (verse 29), "This is the work of God, that you believe in Him whom He sent."

Here Jesus specifies that there is only one work that pleases God, namely, belief in Jesus. Jesus re-emphasizes this in verse 35. "I am the bread of life. He who comes to Me shall never hunger, and he who believes in Me shall never thirst." Notice the imperative is to "come to Me" and "believe in Me." Jesus repeats the thrust of His message in verse 40 where He states — "And this is the will of Him who sent Me, that everyone who sees the Son and believes in Him may have everlasting life; and I will raise him up at the last day."

The Bread of Life

Jesus could not be clearer — by coming to Him and trusting in Him we will receive eternal life. At this point in the narrative, the Jews complained about Him because He said: "I am the bread which came down from heaven" (verse 41). Jesus responds to their murmuring in verses 42 through 58, where He states that He is indeed the "living bread" and that they must eat His flesh and drink His blood to obtain eternal life. However, let's remember the context of this statement. First, Jesus contrasts Himself with the manna that rained down on their fathers and sustained them for their journey. But their fathers have since died. But Jesus now offers Himself as the living bread, causing those who eat of Him to live forever.

Jesus is not the perishable manna that their descendants ate in the wilderness, He is the eternal bread of life that lives forever. Only by partaking in His everlasting life can we hope to live with Him forever. This contrast strengthens His main message, which is recorded in verse 47 where Jesus says, "Most assuredly, I say to you, he who believes in Me has everlasting life." Notice, Jesus said that as soon as we believe in Him we have—present tense— eternal life. It is not something we aim at or hope we might attain in the future, but rather, something we receive immediately upon believing.

When Jesus said these words, He was in the synagogue in Capernaum (verse 59), and He had neither bread nor wine. Therefore Jesus was either commanding cannibalism or He was speaking figuratively. If He was speaking literally, then He would be directly contradicting God the Father: **"You shall not eat flesh with its life, that is, its blood"** (Genesis 9:4). Therefore, because Jesus Himself said, **"The Scripture cannot be broken"** (John 10:35), He must be speaking metaphorically. And that is exactly how He explains His own words in the subsequent verses.

The Flesh Profits Nothing

After this, in verse 60, we find that many of His disciples said—"This is a hard saying; who can understand it?" Jesus was aware of their complaints and He responded in verses 61 through 64 saying—"Does this offend you? What then if you should see the Son of Man ascend where He was before? **It is the Spirit who gives life; the flesh profits nothing. The words that I speak to you are spirit, and they are life.** But there are some of you who do not believe." Wait a minute, the flesh profits nothing! I thought Jesus said we must eat His flesh? Yet, if the flesh profits nothing, Jesus must be speaking in spiritual terms. And that is exactly what He says—"The words that I speak to you are spirit."

Jesus uses the exact same Greek word for flesh (*sarx*) as He did in the preceding verses. Therefore we must conclude that eating His literal flesh profits nothing! If the Lord Himself sets the context of the dialogue, we would do well to hear Him. He said that the words that He speaks are spirit and that the flesh profits nothing.

If that isn't clear enough, Peter's words allow no room for doubt. Immediately following the dialogue with the Jews, in which some disciples went away, Jesus said to the twelve apostles, "Do you also want to go away?" (verse 67). Peter's response is profound. His reply to Jesus is recorded in verse 68. "Lord, to whom shall we go? You have the words of eternal life. Also we have come to believe and know that You are the Christ, the Son of the living God." Amazing! Peter did not say we have come to believe that we must eat Your flesh to live. He said that we know You are the Christ, and we have come to believe in You as the Christ. This is the confession of faith that leads to eternal life, not eating Jesus' flesh and drinking His blood. It also agrees with the totality of Scripture. Here is a brief sampling:

> If you confess with your mouth the Lord Jesus and believe in your heart that God has raised Him from the dead, you will be saved (Romans 10:9).
>
> What must I do to be saved?...Believe on the Lord Jesus Christ, and you will be saved (Acts 16:30, 31).
>
> He who believes in the Son has everlasting life (John 3:36).

Spiritual Sense

In John chapter 6, Jesus clearly contrasted the temporary benefits of the physical manna with the eternal benefits of life in the Spirit. This theme is repeated throughout the Word of God. All through the Bible, the limited and temporary benefits of the flesh are contrasted with the infinite and eternal benefits of the Spirit. Consuming manna, even manna from heaven, has limited value. However, receiving Christ's life, by placing our trust and hope in Him, has infinite value. Romans chapter 8 explains this truth:

> There is therefore now no condemnation to those who are in Christ Jesus, who do not walk according to the flesh, but according to the Spirit. ...For those who live according to the flesh set their minds on the things of the flesh, but those who live according to the Spirit, the things of the Spirit. For to be carnally minded is death, but to be spiritually minded is life and peace. ...So then, those who are in the flesh cannot please God. But you are not in the flesh but in the Spirit, if indeed the Spirit of God dwells in you. Now if anyone does not have the Spirit of Christ, he is not His (Romans 8:1, 5, 6, 8, 9).

Jesus' Seven "I AM" Statements

In addition to Jesus' teaching in John chapter 6, we get additional insight into His message by reading John's entire Gospel, and we begin to fully understand what Jesus meant when He said "I am the bread of life." In John's Gospel, Jesus makes seven "I am" statements. These seven are listed below.

John 6:35	I am the bread of life
John 8:12	I am the light of the world
John 10:9	I am the door

John 10:11   I am the good shepherd

John 11:25   I am the resurrection and the life

John 14:6   I am the way, the truth, and the life

John 15:5   I am the vine

Believers should love these seven "I am" statements. Not only is Jesus claiming to be God, but He is defining who God is. Back in the Book of Exodus, Moses asks God what His name is. [17] God responds to Moses by saying, "My name is I AM." God is the self-existent One. This I AM in the Hebrew is the name of God, the YHWH where we get "Yahweh" and "Jehovah".

And in John's Gospel, Jesus expounds and explains who God is. If your soul is hungering, Jesus would say: I am the bread of life. If you're seeking illumination and understanding, Jesus would say: I am the light of the world. Are you looking for the entrance into abundant life? Jesus would say: I am the door. Do you need guidance and protection? Jesus would say: I am the good shepherd. Are you seeking eternal life? Jesus would say: I am the resurrection and the life. Jesus knows your needs better than you do. Whatever your need, Jesus would say: I am the way, the truth, and the life. I am the vine. If you abide in Me, I will supply all your needs.

What Jesus is saying in John chapter 6 and throughout the Gospel of John is: I am all you need. I created you and I know and understand what you need to be fully satisfied and it is Me. Jesus is our all in all. No matter what we think we need, Jesus, alone can supply our true need. By studying the entire Gospel of John, we see clearly that Jesus is not proclaiming Himself to be literal bread, any more than He is proclaiming Himself to be a literal vine or

---

[17] Exodus 3:11-15

a wooden door. Rather, He is affirming that as our God and Creator, He, and He alone, is all we need. Understanding the whole counsel of God is crucial.

John Chapter 6: Unrelated to the Last Supper

Before leaving chapter 6 of John's Gospel, we must realize that this chapter does not deal directly with the Last Supper, or with the doctrine of the Eucharist. That's worth repeating. John chapter 6 has nothing to do with the Last Supper! Remember, Jesus had neither bread nor wine in this narrative and He never even mentions wine. And while proponents of transubstantiation often refer to these verses to support their doctrine, nowhere in this chapter does Jesus give the disciples instruction on how to celebrate Communion, nor is the Last Supper described here. Therefore we must acknowledge that this is a separate event.

John deals with the Last Supper starting in chapter 13, but chapter 6 is a separate subject. In chapter 6, Jesus never even alludes to a procedure to follow concerning the Communion meal, nor does He tell His disciples to institute a priesthood that will consecrate bread and turn it into His literal flesh. Nor does He teach here or anywhere in the Bible, to worship His body and blood under the appearance of bread.

John Chapter 13

In the thirteenth chapter of John's Gospel, the events of the Last Supper are given. In verses 2 and 4 we read — "And supper being ended...[Jesus] rose from supper and laid aside His garments, took a towel and girded Himself." So we see that by this time in John's account Jesus had already blessed the bread, broke it and said, "This is My body which is given for you" (Luke 22:19).

What is interesting in John's account of the Last Supper, is that after Jesus blessed the bread and said, "This is My body," He referred to the blessed and consecrated bread as mere bread. Verse 26 states: "Jesus answered, 'It is he whom I shall give a piece of bread when I have dipped it.' And having dipped the bread, He gave it to Judas Iscariot, the son of Simon." Did Jesus lose track of what He was doing? Did He misspeak? No. According to Jesus' own words, the bread remained bread even after being blessed.

In fact, John chapter 13 mentions bread five times. In each case, the blessed bread is referred to as plain bread. [18] For instance, in verse 27 we read—"Now after the piece of bread, Satan entered him [Judas]." The Word of God tells us that Satan entered Judas right after receiving the bread. There in no indication that John believed in or taught transubstantiation.

Matthew, Mark and Luke

Matthew 26:17-29, Mark 14:12-25, and Luke 22:7-23 give parallel accounts of what took place on the night before Jesus was crucified. In Luke 22:15-19 Jesus said to His disciples:

> "With fervent desire I have desired to eat this Passover with you before I suffer; for I say to you, I will no longer eat of it until it is fulfilled in the kingdom of God." Then He took the cup, and gave thanks, and said, "Take this and divide it among yourselves; for I say to you, I will not drink of the fruit of the vine until the kingdom of God comes." And He took bread, gave thanks and broke it, and gave it to them, saying, "This is My body which is given for you; do this in remembrance of Me."

----

[18] John 13:18, 26, 27, 30

Previously, we've given several examples showing that God often uses figurative language to describe Himself and to illustrate a spiritual truth. There are many biblical reasons why Jesus' words at the Last Supper were meant to be taken figuratively. The remainder of this chapter will examine why.

The Passover Lamb

Exodus chapters 12 and 13 describe the events of the original Passover. Each year the Jews were to observe the Passover as a memorial of their deliverance out of bondage. On this night a lamb without blemish was slain and its blood applied to the door posts and lintel of each believer's house. The blood of the lamb covered those who trusted in the Lord. All who applied the lamb's blood would be spared, while those who ignored God's warning would be destroyed.

The Scriptures clearly explain that "For indeed Christ, our Passover, was sacrificed for us" (1 Corinthians 5:7). When John the Baptist first saw Jesus he proclaimed: "Behold! The Lamb of God who takes away the sin of the world!" (John 1:29). Jesus fulfilled each and every Old Testament type that pointed to the coming Messiah. This included the Passover Lamb. During the Last Supper, Jesus was declaring that He Himself would become our substitutionary lamb. He would die in our place. All who repented of their sins and placed their trust in Him would be delivered from the bondage of sin and death.

Of course during the Last Supper Jesus did not become a literal lamb, nor did the bread become His literal body. To the Jewish believers in attendance it would have been clear that Jesus Himself was to be the sacrifice for their sins. Jesus would fulfill the Jewish prophecy that the Messiah would bear our sins in His own body (Isaiah 53:5-12; 1 Peter 2:24). It would be His body that would be killed and

His blood that would be shed for our sins. The Old Testament sacrifices and offerings—which foreshadowed Christ—would be fulfilled in the Son of God. No longer would there be any need to offer sacrifices for our sins. God Himself would once and for all atone for all sins. This is what Jesus meant when He referred to the Passover elements as His body and blood.

The next day His body was indeed broken and His blood was poured out for the sins of the world. His command to believers is "do this in remembrance of Me." Celebrating Communion is therefore a memorial, not a re-sacrificing of Jesus. At the Last Supper Jesus did not institute a priesthood. He in no way ordained transubstantiation. And He definitely did not condone an ongoing sacrificial system. No, the good news is that:

> For by one offering He has perfected forever those who are being sanctified...there is no longer an offering for sin (Hebrews 10:14, 18).

As the Jews celebrated Passover in remembrance of their deliverance from the bondage of slavery, we celebrate the Lord's Supper in remembrance of our deliverance from the bondage of sin. Jesus is our Passover Lamb, though He is not a literal lamb.

Jesus' One Body is in Heaven

We are told in Mark 16:19 that "[Jesus] was received up into heaven, and sat down at the right hand of God." Jesus ascended bodily to be at the right hand of the Father. Peter says it this way: "[Jesus] has gone into heaven and is at the right hand of God" (1 Peter 3:22). Jesus' one and only glorified body is in heaven. This makes sense when we remember that He said, "Do this in remembrance of Me." If Jesus' body, blood, soul and divinity is with us in the Eucharist, the words "do this in remembrance of Me" would make no sense. A memorial service is not held for someone who is in attendance, but rather for someone who has departed.

Now, of course, Jesus is God and "God is Spirit, and those who worship Him must worship in spirit and truth" (John 4:24). Jesus is with us spiritually and He is omnipresent (present everywhere), so He is with all of us right now—wherever we may be. But His glorified body is in heaven. "After He [Jesus] had offered one sacrifice for sins forever, sat down at the right hand of God, from that time waiting till His enemies are made His footstool. For by one offering He has perfected forever those who are being sanctified" (Hebrews 10:12-14). It is clear that Jesus' body is in heaven and we are to remember what He did for us on the cross by celebrating Communion.

The Acts of the Early Church

The early church celebrated Communion frequently and their actions are recorded in the Book of Acts. Let's look at how the apostles and disciples celebrated Communion after Jesus' ascension. In the Book of Acts we read:

> And they continued steadfastly in the apostles' doctrine and fellowship, and breaking of bread, and in prayers (Acts 2:42).

> So continuing daily with one accord in the temple, and breaking bread from house to house, they ate their food with gladness (Acts 2:46).

> And when he [Paul] had said these things, he took bread and gave thanks to God in the presence of them all; and when he had broken it he began to eat. Then they were all encouraged, and also took food themselves (Acts 27:35, 36).

The Lord's apostles, the very same ones that were present at the Last Supper, broke bread daily, celebrating

Communion, and not once did they refer to the bread as the literal body, blood, soul and divinity of Jesus. Even on Sunday, which is the day that the Lord rose, they referred to Communion as mere bread. In a key verse in the Book of Acts, we read: "Now on the first day of the week, when the disciples came together to break bread..." (Acts 20:7).

Notice that the disciples broke bread on Sunday in remembrance of Jesus' death and resurrection. Search as we might, there is no hint in the entire Book of Acts that the disciples considered the Communion service as anything but a memorial service. This does not lessen its importance, rather it emphasizes that the reason for the Communion celebration is to remember the completed work of the cross and that Jesus is now in heaven as our triumphant King!

God Does Not Dwell in Temples Made with Hands

What is interesting in the Book of Acts is the repeated, emphatic statement made by the disciples that God does not dwell in temples! **"However, the Most High does not dwell in temples made with hands..."** (Acts 7:48).

> [Paul said] Men of Athens, I perceive that in all things you are very religious; for as I was passing through and considering the objects of your worship, I even found an altar with this inscription: TO THE UNKNOWN GOD. Therefore, the One whom you worship without knowing, Him I proclaim to you: God, who made the world and everything in it, since He is Lord of heaven and earth, does not dwell in temples made with hands. Nor is He worshiped with men's hands, as though He needed anything (Acts 17:22-25).

This truth is also echoed in the Book of Hebrews: "For Christ has not entered the holy places made with hands...but into heaven itself, now to appear in the presence of God for us" (Hebrews 9:24).

The Eucharistic tabernacle is a "holy place" made with human hands! Yet, the Bible states that Christ is not there but in heaven. In addition, the Greek word for *temple* is *naos*, which can also be translated as *shrine* or a place of worship. God says He doesn't dwell there, yet the Catholic Church insists that Jesus is present in all the Eucharistic tabernacles of the world. The Communion Host is made with men's hands, yet, the Bible states that God is NOT worshipped with men's hands (Acts 17:25).

Abstain from Blood

Furthermore, the apostles also commanded believers to abstain from blood. In the Book of Acts, we find that the apostles and elders came together to consider certain Jewish customs that had crept into the early church. Their decision, stated by James, is as follows:

> Therefore, I judge that we should not trouble those from among the Gentiles who are turning to God, but that we write to them to abstain from things polluted by idols, from sexual immorality, from things strangled, and from blood (Acts 15:19, 20).

If the original apostles and disciples repeatedly commanded new believers to abstain from blood (see also Acts 15:29; 21:25), why does the Roman Catholic Church encourage followers to eat Jesus' body and blood? If the consecrated Communion Host becomes Jesus literal body, BLOOD, soul, and divinity, then partaking in Communion goes against the Holy Spirit's command to abstain from blood. This is a direct contradiction.

From the very beginning, God commanded mankind to abstain from blood — "But you shall not eat flesh with its life, that is, its blood" (Genesis 9:4). Moses reiterated this command, "No one among you shall eat blood, nor shall any stranger who dwells among you eat blood" (Leviticus 17:12). "You shall not eat anything with the blood, nor shall you practice divination or soothsaying" (Leviticus 19:26). The prophets repeated God's command "...do not sin against the LORD by eating with the blood" (1 Samuel 14:34).

In the Book of Acts, the Jewish disciples were confirming what God — who cannot lie and does not change — commanded in the Old Testament. Therefore, only a figurative interpretation of the Last Supper is in harmony with the whole counsel of God.

First Corinthians 11

Some proponents of the Eucharist argue that First Corinthians 11 supports transubstantiation. They refer to verse 29 that states: "For he who eats and drinks in an unworthy manner eats and drinks judgment to himself, not discerning the Lord's body." A thorough read of First Corinthians 11, reveals that the Corinthians were not making the proper distinction between Communion and common meals. Not discerning the Lord's body meant not discerning in the bread and wine the symbols of Christ's body and blood, but partaking of them irreverently, as if it were a common feast.

It is evident that this was the leading offense of the Corinthians. Those who were eating and drinking in an unworthy manner were getting drunk and selfishly eating before others in the body of Christ. Paul states this as the problem in verses 20 and 21. There is no indication that the apostle Paul believed in or taught transubstantiation.

In fact, Paul repeatedly refers to the blessed bread as normal bread after it had been blessed. [19] Paul states in verse 26 — "For as often as you eat this bread and drink this cup, you proclaim the Lord's death till He comes."

Notice also that Paul explains that we are to celebrate the Lord's Supper "till He comes". The words "till He comes" pre-supposes that the Lord has ascended on high. [20] Therefore the Lord's Supper is in remembrance of His death and resurrection *until He returns*. This agrees with what Jesus ordained when He said, "Do this in remembrance of Me" (Luke 22:19).

Finally, it is apparent that First Corinthians 11 uses figurative language to describe Communion. The cup is referred to figuratively: "This cup is the new covenant in My blood..." (1 Corinthians 11:25). Of course the cup was not the actual covenant but symbolic of it. "For as often as you eat this bread and drink this cup, you proclaim the Lord's death till He comes." (1 Corinthians 11:26). Surely we are not to drink the cup. This is a figurative reference to the wine inside the cup.

Finished Work

Perhaps the most disturbing aspect of this Catholic doctrine is that Christ is being re-sacrificed daily by thousands of Catholic priests. And that by receiving the Eucharist a Catholic can obtain forgiveness of sins. In other words, the Catholic Church teaches that the Eucharist is a sacrificial offering able to atone for sins. Therefore, Christ is ever suffering and dying each time a priest consecrates the wafer. Here is how the Catechism explains it:

---

[19] 1 Corinthians 11:26-28
[20] 1 Peter 3:21, 22; Matthew 26:64; Romans 8:34; Ephesians 1:20; Colossians 3:1; Hebrews 1:3; 9:24, 25; 12:2. Many Scripture verses state that Jesus' one and only body is in heaven.

As sacrifice, the Eucharist is also offered in reparation for the sins of the living and the dead and to
obtain spiritual or temporal benefits from God. [21]

Every time this mystery is celebrated, "the work of
our redemption is carried on." [22]

The Eucharist is thus a sacrifice because it *re-
presents* (makes present) the sacrifice of the cross. [23]

This teaching directly contradicts the Word of God.
When Jesus died on the cross He proclaimed: "It is finished!" (John 19:30). The Greek word used is *tetelestai*. It
was a Greek accounting term that meant "paid in full".
The work for our salvation is complete! Christ purchased
our redemption once and for all on the cross. Jesus is not
being perpetually sacrificed in the Eucharist as the Catholic Church teaches. Partaking in the Eucharist does not appease God, nor does it atone for sin. If you are a Catholic,
then the following verses can be transforming and revolu-
tionary if you will simply take God at His word.

For Christ has not entered the holy places made
with hands, which are copies of the true, but into
heaven itself, now to appear in the presence of God
for us; not that He should offer Himself often, as
the high priest enters the Most Holy Place every
year with blood of another—He then would have
had to suffer often since the foundation of the
world; but now, once at the end of the ages, He has
appeared to put away sin by the sacrifice of Himself. And as it is appointed for men to die once, but
after this the judgment, **so Christ was offered once
to bear the sins of many**. To those who eagerly

---

21 Catechism of the Catholic Church, para. 1414, page 395.
22 Ibid., para. 1405, page 393.
23 Ibid., para. 1366, page 380.

wait for Him He will appear a second time, apart from sin, for salvation (Hebrews 9:24-28).

And every priest stands ministering daily and offering repeatedly the same sacrifices, which can never take away sins. But this Man, after He had offered one sacrifice for sins forever, sat down at the right hand of God, from that time waiting till His enemies are made His footstool. For by one offering He has perfected forever those who are being sanctified. ...**there is no longer an offering for sin** (Hebrews 10:11-14, 18).

Knowing that Christ, having been raised from the dead, dies no more. Death no longer has dominion over Him. For the death that He died, He died to sin once for all; but the life that He lives, He lives to God (Romans 6:9-10).

For Christ also suffered once for sins, the just for the unjust, that He might bring us to God, being put to death in the flesh but made alive by the Spirit (1 Peter 3:18).

Incarnation, Ascension, Second Coming

There are many other Scriptures that refute transubstantiation. For example, transubstantiation contradicts the biblical doctrine of the incarnation and ascension. The Bible tells us that Jesus had one, and only one, body prepared for Him by the Father, "a body you have prepared for Me" (Hebrews 10:5). "Inasmuch then as the children have partaken of flesh and blood, He Himself likewise shared in the same, that through death He might destroy him who had the power of death, that is, the devil" (Hebrews 2:14).

Furthermore the Scriptures tell us clearly that Jesus' one and only glorified body is in heaven: "Jesus Christ...has gone into heaven and is at the right hand of God..." (1 Peter 3:21, 22). "If then you were raised with Christ, seek those things which are above, where Christ is, sitting at the right hand of God" (Colossians 3:1). "[Jesus] who descended is also the One who ascended far above all the heavens..." (Ephesians 4:10). There are many, many verses that reiterate that Jesus' one body is in heaven. [24] If Jesus' only body is in heaven, then it is not in thousands of tabernacles around the world.

Transubstantiation also contradicts the Bible's teaching concerning the Second Coming of Christ. Many Catholics who believe that Jesus Christ will physically and visibly return to earth also believe that Christ will come back first in His "Eucharistic form". [25] However, once again the Bible clearly refutes this notion:

> Now when He had spoken these things, while they watched, He was taken up, and a cloud received Him out of their sight. And while they looked steadfastly toward heaven as He went up, behold, two men stood by them in white apparel, who also said, "Men of Galilee, why do you stand gazing up into heaven? This same Jesus, who was taken up from you into heaven, will so come in like manner as you saw Him go into heaven." (Acts 1:9-11).

> Then they will see the Son of Man coming in the clouds with great power and glory (Mark 13:26).

> Behold, He is coming with clouds, and every eye will see Him, even they who pierced Him (Revelation 1:7).

---

[24] Matthew 26:64; Mark 14:62; 16:19; Luke 22:69; Acts 2:33; 7:55-56; Romans 8:34; Ephesians 1:20; 2:16; Colossians 3:1; Hebrews 1:3; 8:1; 9:24, 25; 10:12; 12:2; 1 Peter 3:22.
[25] Refer to chapter 11, "The Eucharistic Reign of Christ."

Behold, the Lord comes with ten thousands of His saints, to execute judgment on all... (Jude 1:14-15).

Jesus ascended bodily and He will return in His glorified body—not in the form of a wafer. Furthermore, the Bible never ascribes more than one location to His physical body at any given time—neither should we. When Jesus returns in His glorified body every eye will see Him. Transubstantiation is therefore unbiblical.

In the final book of the Bible, Christ's Second Coming is described and confirmed as follows:

Now I saw heaven opened, and behold, a white horse. And He who sat on him was called Faithful and True, and in righteousness He judges and makes war. His eyes were like a flame of fire, and on His head were many crowns. He had a name written that no one knew except Himself. He was clothed with a robe dipped in blood, and His name is called The Word of God. And the armies in heaven, clothed in fine linen, white and clean, followed Him on white horses (Revelation 19:11-14).

Mystery and Miracles

The Catholic Church refers to the Mass as a mystery. However, the Bible never refers to Communion as a mystery, nor should we. Remember the warning in Scripture not to corrupt the pure and simple truth of the gospel: "But I fear, lest somehow, as the serpent deceived Eve by his craftiness, so your minds may be corrupted from the simplicity that is in Christ" (2 Corinthians 11:3).

When the priest consecrates the Host nothing happens. The bread still looks like bread, feels like bread, smells like bread, and tastes like bread. There is not a single miracle in the Bible where all outward evidences reveal that nothing happened. Biblical miracles are always tangible and practical. Moses really parted the Red Sea — he didn't ask the people to cross before parting it. Elijah actually called down literal fire to the horror of the false prophets. Jesus literally healed the sick, cleansed the lepers, and raised the dead. God has never dealt with mankind using virtual "miracles".

Some may point to reports of Eucharistic miracles as evidence that the consecrated Host is the literal body and blood of Christ. However, the Bible warns of just such a deception occurring in the last days:

> For false christs and false prophets will rise and show great signs and wonders to deceive, if possible, even the elect. "See, I have told you beforehand. "Therefore if they say to you, 'Look, He is in the desert!' do not go out; or 'Look, He is in the inner rooms!' do not believe it." (Matthew 24:24-26).

The Eucharistic Jesus is a false christ whom many false prophets claim is in the inner rooms of thousands of Catholic churches. Furthermore, as we shall document, many lying signs and wonders are accompanying Eucharistic exposition and adoration. Not surprisingly, the Bible reveals that these tangible Eucharistic miracles have a demonic origin.

The "Unbloody" Sacrifice

The Catholic Church teaches that the Eucharist is an "unbloody sacrifice" in which Christ is actually "immolated" or offered as the victim. In fact the term "Host" is derived from the Latin word for victim. Therefore the offering of the Host is the perpetuation of the sacrifice of Christ in an unbloody manner to make satisfaction for sins. Yet the Bible states succinctly that there is no forgiveness of sins without the shedding of blood:

...without shedding of blood there is no remission (Hebrews 9:22).

For the life of the flesh is in the blood, and I have given it to you upon the altar to make atonement for your souls; for it is the blood that makes atonement for the soul (Leviticus 17:11).

Furthermore, in the Scriptures, we never find mention of bread or wine as a sacrifice. In addition, at the Last Supper the Lord took bread and wine at a table, not an altar. In the Bible, sacrifices were made on an altar. In fact, God commanded the Jews that there was to be only one altar. [26] Certainly Jesus' Jewish disciples knew this. As God, Jesus would not contradict Himself. Tables are for eating, altars are for sacrificing.

Eternal Consequences

Clearly, the Catholic doctrine of the Eucharist is contrary to God's Word. But just how serious is this doctrinal error? Is it serious enough to determine one's eternal destiny? Ironically, the following quote from former Protestant Peter Kreeft, now a strong proponent of the Catholic Eucharist, accurately expresses the significance and consequence of submitting to this belief:

What a point of division the Eucharist is! One of the two sides is very, very wrong. I said before that if Protestants are right, Catholics are making the terrible mistake of idolatrously adoring bread and wine as God. But if Catholics are right, Protestants are making the just-as-terrible mistake of refusing to adore Christ where He is and are missing out on

---

[26] Deuteronomy 12:5-14; Exodus 20:24-26; Joshua 22:16

the most ontologically real union with Christ that is possible in this life, in Holy Communion. [27]

Consider the repercussions of what Kreeft has written. If Catholics are wrong in their belief in and worship of the Eucharist, then they are guilty of idolatry. Therefore, they are directly violating the first and second commandments (Exodus 20:3-5).

It is imperative that we believe in and direct all worship toward the true Jesus of the Bible. Jesus warned that there would be many false christs. That being the case, shouldn't all professing Christians search the Scriptures diligently to determine the truth? This is God's desire. "And you will seek Me and find Me, when you search for Me with all your heart" (Jeremiah 29:13). "Man shall not live by bread alone, but by every word of God" (Luke 4:4). "Sanctify them by Your truth. Your word is truth" (John 17:17).

---

[27] Peter Kreeft, *Ecumenical Jihad*, Ignatius Press, San Francisco, 1994, pages 159, 160.

Chapter Five
The Monstrance

The first four chapters of this book have documented the distinct significance and critical importance that the Eucharist has in faith and practice for millions of Roman Catholics. In addition, documentation has been provided that reveals the tremendous importance the Catholic Church has placed on the Eucharist as a means to evangelize non-Catholics. Finally, using Catholic sources, transubstantiation has been thoroughly discussed in light of the Bible.

The fact that the Catholic Church accepts and promotes the idea that the presence of Jesus Christ manifests in a consecrated wafer can not be disputed. In addition, it is claimed that only validly ordained Catholic priests have the power to perform the mystical procedure called transubstantiation. Further, those who receive the wafer have "Christ" in them because they have eaten the body of "Jesus." These teachings are foundational and necessary for someone to become a genuine Catholic according to the Catholic faith.

While Catholic theologians claim these ideas are supported by Scripture, the Scriptures reveal that worshipping a piece of bread is clearly a distortion of what the Bible teaches. Jesus instructed His disciples to take bread and wine as a remembrance of the sacrifice that He would make that was fulfilled by His death upon the cross. Salvation must always be understood in light of the work that Jesus completed on the cross, not on a ritual that can be repeated over and over and is dependent on a select group of individuals who have the mystical power to command His appearance in the form of a wafer.

It is certain then, that the Eucharistic Christ is the "Jesus" that is promoted by the Catholic Church. If this teaching is in error it is obvious there are serious consequences.

But there is another aspect of the Eucharistic Christ that needs to be addressed. Not only does this "Christ" appear on the altar in the form of bread and wine, the Catholic Church also teaches and promotes that this "presence" can be contained and adored in a vessel called a monstrance.

Not a single reference to the word *monstrance* can be found in the Bible. In fact, the idea that God can be contained and displayed in a man-made vessel directly contradicts the Word of God: "God, who made the world and everything in it, since He is Lord of heaven and earth, does not dwell in temples made with hands" (Acts 17:24).

Displaying Jesus?

I can vividly recall the first time I came across the term monstrance. During the time period when I was doing research for my book *New Wine and the Babylonian Vine,* I was given a number of booklets and pamphlets on the topic of Marian apparitions, (supernatural appearances of the Virgin Mary).

In one of these booklets I came across a photo of an interesting object that I had never seen before. It was called a monstrance. The appearance of this monstrance immediately caught my attention—a cross, a sunburst and a moon decorating an object that had a circular glass window that appeared to be the opening to a central chamber that contained a wafer.

Later I discovered that the monstrance was an essential component of the Mass. It was the container that had been devised by the Catholic Church to display consecrated Hosts for the purpose of adoring "Jesus." According to one Catholic source the monstrance is defined as:

> A vessel usually made of gold or precious metal which is used for the exposition of the Blessed Sacrament. The principal part is a circular glass through which the consecrated Host can be viewed. Surrounding this circular glass is a metal sunburst of golden "rays." A cross might surmount the vessel, which stands on a pedestal and is supported by a circular base. A crescent-shaped device (lunette) or a double circle of gold or metal gilt by means of which the Host is held securely upright when exposed in a monstrance. [1]

The Catholic Encyclopedia and the Monstrance

If there is no mention of the monstrance in the Bible, what do Catholics teach about the origin of the monstrance and how did the acceptance of the monstrance come about? To answer this question, we can turn to *The Catholic Encyclopedia*:

> Monstrance—a tower-shaped vessel for preserving and exhibiting relics and the Blessed Sacrament sometimes, lastly, like today, it was the name of the

---

[1] Joan Carol Cruz, *Eucharistic Miracles*, Tan Books and Publishers, Rockford, IL, 1987, page xiii, Imprimatur, Phillip M. Hannan, Archbishop of New Orleans, April 25, 1986, pages xxi–xxii.

vessel holding the pyx. That is, at the present time
in ecclesiastical usage it is only the name for the receptacle or case placed upon the table of the high
altar or of another altar in which the vessels containing the Blessed Sacrament as the ciborium,
monstrance, custodia, are kept. As a rule, in cathe-
drals and monastic churches it is not set upon the
high altar but upon a side altar, or the altar of a
special sacramentary chapel; this is to be done both
on account of the reverence due the Holy Sacrament and to avoid impeding the course of the
ceremonies in solemn functions at the high altar.
On the other hand it is generally to be placed upon
the high altar in parish churches as the most befit-
ting position ("Cærem. ep.", I, xii, No. 8; "Rit. rom.",
tit. IV, i, no. 6; S.C. Episc., 10 February, 1579).[2]

The Catholic Encyclopedia provides further insight regarding the origin and history of the monstrance:

In the Middle Ages there was no uniform custom
in regard to the place where the Blessed Sacrament
was kept. The Fourth Latern Council and many
provincial and diocesan synods held in the Middle
Ages require only that the Host be kept in a secure,
well-fastened receptacle. At the most they demand
that it be put in a clean, conspicuous place. Only a
few synods designate the spot more closely, as the
Synods of Cologne (1281) and of Münster (1279)
which commanded that it was to be kept above the
altar and protected by locking with a key. In gen-

---

[2] The *Catholic Encyclopedia, Volume XI*, Copyright 1911, Robert
Appleton Company, Online Edition, Copyright 2003 by K.
Knight *Nihil Obstat, February 1, 1911*. Remy Lafort, S.TA.D., Cen-
sor Imprimatur, John Cardinal Farley, Archbishop of New York.

eral, four main methods of preserving the Blessed Sacrament may be distinguished in medieval times:

- in a cabinet in the sacristy, a custom that is connected with early Christian usage;

- in a cupboard in the wall of the choir or in a projection from one of the walls which was constructed like a tower, was called Sacrament-House, and sometimes reached up to the vaulting;

- in a dove or pyx, surrounded by a cover or receptacle and generally surmounted by a small baldachino, which hung over the altar by a chain or cord;

- lastly, upon the altar table, either in the pyx alone or in a receptacle similar to a tabernacle, or in a small cupboard arranged in the reredos or predella of the altar.

Further insight is provided from *The Catholic Encyclopedia* on the topic of how devotion for the Blessed Sacrament came about:

The idea of exposing the Blessed Sacrament for veneration in a monstrance appears to have been first evolved at the end of the thirteenth or the beginning of the fourteenth century. When the elevation of the Host at Mass was introduced in the early years of the thirteenth century, probably as a form of protest against the theological views of Peter the Chanter, the idea by degrees took firm hold of the popular mind that special virtue and merit were attached to the act of looking at the Blessed Sacrament. To such extremes did this prepossession go, that the seeing of the Host at the moment of the elevation was judged to be the most vital part of attendance at Mass.

On certain churches in Spain a screen of black velvet was held up behind the altar in order that the priest's hands and the Host might be more easily seen from afar; in others strict injunctions were given to the thurifer that he should on no account allow the smoke of the thurible to obstruct the view of the Host. Furthermore, we read that when men were dying and were unable on account of vomiting or any other cause to receive Holy Viaticum, the Blessed Sacrament was brought to them and held up before them to look at. Indeed, a virtual prohibition of this practice stands to this day amongst the rubrics of the "Rituale Romanum."

Under the influence of this idea, the Blessed Sacrament in the processions which became common after the institution of the feast of Corpus Christi in 1246, came by degrees to be carried in transparent vessels, resembling our present monstrances. Moreover, a custom grew up, especially in Germany, of keeping the Blessed Sacrament continually exposed to view in churches. It was forbidden by many synods, but a sort of compromise was arrived at through the construction of the *Sakramentshäuschen* of which so many examples still exist in central Europe.

These tabernacles, of great height and imposing appearance, were erected in the most conspicuous part of the church, and there the Blessed Sacrament was reserved in a monstrance behind a metal door of lattice-work which allowed a more or less free view of the interior. It was thus that the practice developed, though partly kept in check by synodal decrees, of adding solemnity to any function, even the Mass itself, by exposing the Blessed Sacrament during its continuance. [3]

In this chapter, we have examined the topic of the monstrance and the role it plays in understanding the Eucharist and the Eucharistic Christ. It should be apparent by now that a faith that is based on tradition and not on the Bible, can open the door to serious deception, the very kind of deception that the Bible warns will result in people going to hell.

In the next chapter we will examine the topic of how the Eucharist is being promoted as a means for evangelization to bring people into the Catholic Church. Once more we will examine current trends supported by various articles from Catholic sources. In so doing, we will learn more about the Eucharistic Jesus that can be displayed in a monstrance or contained in a tabernacle.

---

[3] Ibid.

Chapter Six
The New Evangelization

When Christians speak of the term evangelization, they are usually referring to efforts to fulfill the Great Commission. Just before ascending to heaven Jesus commissioned every believer to proclaim the good news when He said: "Go into all the world and preach the gospel to every creature." [1] This gospel of Jesus Christ is very simple. It is a message that even a child can understand.

The gospel is about God's plan to save us from our sins. Since the fall of man, all have been born into this world separated from God our Creator by sin. About two thousand years ago, Jesus Christ, God's Son, supernaturally came to this earth, born of a virgin. While here on earth, Jesus lived a sinless life. He died upon the cross at Calvary, and His blood was shed as a sacrifice for our sins. All those who will accept and believe in Jesus (that is, who Jesus is and what He has done) can enter into a relationship with Jesus, the Creator of the universe. This relationship will then last for eternity. This is the simple gospel.

Unfortunately, Satan has always had an agenda to complicate the gospel or confound people into believing in something less or something more than what the gospel

---

[1] Mark 16:15

message teaches. Paul talked about "another gospel" when he was warning the Corinthians [2] and the Galatians [3] about the dangers of being deceived. Satan is a clever schemer. Deceiving people in the name of the Savior is part of the devil's ultimate plan.

It is important to understand then, that not everything that is labeled "the gospel" is the true gospel. Further, it follows, that the term evangelization, if it is based on a counterfeit gospel, will seduce people into believing they are going to heaven, when instead they may be on their way to hell.

In this chapter we will be dealing with a current program called "The New Evangelization." This program that is being promoted by the Catholic Church is designed to win the world to Christ—the Eucharistic Christ. If the Eucharistic Christ is not the Jesus of the Bible, this would mean the New Evangelization is leading people astray.

This chapter will present the facts about the New Evangelization. You can decide whether or not this program points people to the Jesus of the Bible.

What is the New Evangelization?

While reading a book or an article, have you ever come across a term you had never seen before and suddenly your mind was illuminated? Just as if a light switch was turned on and a darkened room was lit, the significance of what you had read became apparent. Such was the case for me when I came across the phrase the New Evangelization.

I was reading an article published by *Zenit* (The World Seen from Rome) that presented a news item based on

---

[2] 2 Corinthians 11:4
[3] Galatians 1:6

statements made by Pope John Paul II. The article caught my attention because it was about an announcement the pope had made about the Eucharist. The article was titled "Why the Pope Would Write an Encyclical on the Eucharist: To Rekindle Amazement." [4]

While I was already aware the pope had declared the Eucharist to be the focal point for the Catholic Church's missionary vision at the Eucharistic Congress in June of 2000, the idea that the pope had written an Encyclical on the Eucharist to "Rekindle Amazement" in the Eucharist was new to me. I read the article with great interest. The following statement made by the pope was the one that was so enlightening:

> ...the Church will only be able to address the challenge of the new evangelization if she is able to contemplate, and enter into a profound relationship with Christ in the sacrament that makes his presence real. [5]

This was the first time I had heard about the Catholic Church's program called the New Evangelization. Second, this statement helped form a single piece of a puzzle that was now beginning to fall into place. It was obvious this new evangelization program was associated with "a profound relationship with Christ in the sacrament that makes his presence real."

Further, the *Zenit* article gave more details on how the pope wanted to see this program develop:

> I would like to rekindle this Eucharistic amazement by the present Encyclical Letter, in continuity with

---

[4] *Zenit: The World Seen From Rome*, "Why the Pope Would Write an Encyclical on the Eucharist: To Rekindle Amazement," cited April 17, 2003, online posting: www.zenit.org/english.
[5] Ibid.

the Jubilee heritage which I have left to the Church
in the Apostolic Letter Novo Millennio Ineunte and
its Marian crowning, Rosarium Virginis Mariae. To
contemplate the face of Christ, and to contemplate
it with Mary, is the program which I have set before the Church at the dawn of the third millennium, summoning her to put out into the deep on
the sea of history with the enthusiasm of the new
evangelization.

Further, making it crystal clear that the new evangelization program would be tightly associated with the sacrament of the Eucharist, the pope concluded:

> To contemplate Christ involves being able to rec-
> ognize him wherever he manifests himself, in his
> many forms of presence, but above all in the living
> sacrament of his body and his blood. The Church
> draws her life from Christ in the Eucharist, by him
> she is fed and by him she is enlightened.

The Facts about "The New Evangelization"

Of course, one piece of documentation is not sufficient
when presenting a case. In order to find out more about
what this "New Evangelization" program was all about, I
decided to look for more information.

It did not take long to find out that there were many
sources available confirming there was such a program.
One article that was particularly helpful was found on the
EWTN (Eternal Word Television Network) web site. Un-
der a heading "The New Evangelization: Building the
Civilization of Love," I read:

> As the Holy Father entrusts the Third Millennium
> to the Blessed Virgin Mary, EWTN inaugurates it's
> New Evangelization specialty site. This site will be
> forever a work in progress, as we continue to bring

to you information about the Catholic Faith on the 5 continents. We hope that the information on the synods will be a help to those whose mission is to evangelize, a mission which belongs to us at least through prayer. The historical, statistical and devotional material should give every visitor a sense of the universality of the Church and its mission. As well as being an impetus to further the New Evangelization by prayer and action. [6]

Then one additional and very significant statement—

Under the protection of St. Therese of Lisieux, Patroness of the Missions, and Our Lady of Guadalupe, to whom the Pope has committed the New Evangelization, may the Spirit of God bring about the New Pentecost to which the Church looks forward with hope. [7]

This above statement may come as a surprise to Protestant Charismatics who are enthusiastically joining hands with Catholics for the sake of evangelism. The Catholic program is committed to "Our Lady of Guadalupe." Furthermore, it would be good to check out what is meant by the "New Pentecost" [8] that the Catholic Church is expecting. Remember, Paul also warned the Corinthians about

---

[6] "The New Evangelization: Building the Civilization of Love," cited April 2003, online posting: www.ewtn.com/new_evangelization/introduction.htm, Eternal Word Television Network.

[7] Ibid.

[8] Roger Oakland, New Wine and the Babylonian Vine, Understand The Times, Santa Ana, CA, 2002, chapter 18, pages 243-264.

"another spirit" that was associated with "another gospel" and "another Jesus." [9]

New Evangelization Evangelists

Cardinal Ratzinger is one spokesperson for the New Evangelization program that was initiated by the pope. On December 12, 2000, in an address to catechists and religion teachers, Ratzinger spoke about the need for the New Evangelization program. He said:

The Church always evangelizes and has never interrupted the path of evangelization. She celebrates the Eucharistic miracle every day, administers the sacraments, proclaims the word of life — the Word of God and commits herself to the causes of justice and charity. And this evangelization bears fruit: it gives light and joy, it gives the path of light to many people; many others live unknowingly, of the light and the warmth that radiate from this permanent evangelization.

However, we can see a progressive process of de-Christianization and a loss of essential human values, which is worrisome. A large part of today's humanity does not find the Gospel in the permanent evangelization of the Church: That is to say, the convincing response to the question: How to live?

This is why we are searching for, along with the permanent and uninterrupted and never to be interrupted evangelization, a new evangelization, capable of being heard by a world that does not find access to "classic" evangelization. Everyone needs the Gospel; the Gospel is destined to all and

---

[9] 2 Corinthians 11:4

not to a specific circle and this is why we are obliged to look for new ways of bringing the Gospel to all. [10]

These words were spoken by Cardinal Ratzinger in December of 2000, making the pope's statement quoted earlier in this chapter even more significant. If the Catholic Church was "searching for" a method of evangelization for the "new evangelization" in the year 2000, apparently that method has now been discovered and endorsed. Remember, the pope called for a "rekindling of Eucharistic amazement" associated with the New Evangelization.

More Evidence

One more piece of evidence that the Eucharist is a key to understanding the New Evangelization comes from an advertisement I discovered in *Envoy Magazine*. On page 9 of an issue published in 2003 my attention was drawn to the question that formed the heading for the advertisement: "Will you answer our Holy Father's call for the New Evangelization?" [11] Beneath the title, the following information was presented:

The gift of the Catholic faith is of such awesome magnitude that we have an important duty to share it. The Children of the Father Foundation, a non-profit, Catholic evangelization apostolate, is giving away over 100,000 free books, tapes and pamphlets this year. There are three ways you can help this powerful evangelization effort:

---

[10] Online posting: www.ewtn.com/new_evangelization/Ratzinger.htm, Cardinal Ratzinger address on December 12, 2000.

[11] *Envoy Magazine,* Volume 7.2, Granville, OH, 2003, page 9.

1. Distribute this free literature to your parish, co-workers, family, friends, etc.

2. Join our informal prayer group "Friends of Our Lady."

3. Help us purchase additional evangelization materials for free distribution.

However, what really caught my attention was the front cover of a book that was shown as part of this advertisement. It was titled *The Most Blessed Sacrament: Our Lord is truly present: Body, Soul and Divinity to make you happy now and for all Eternity!* by author Fr. Stephano Manelli, O.F.M. On the front cover of this book was a monstrance. In the location where the wafer would normally be found there was an actual face — supposedly the face of "Jesus."

I ordered a copy of this booklet that was being promoted as a tool for the New Evangelization available from the Children of the Father Foundation. As I read through the booklet a number of significant statements were noted. For example:

Let us ask the question: What is the Eucharist? It is *God among us*. It is the Lord Jesus present in the tabernacles of our churches with His Body, Blood, Soul and Divinity. It is Jesus veiled under the appearance of bread, but really and physically present in the consecrated Host, so that He dwells in our midst, works within us and for us, and is at our disposal. The Eucharistic Jesus is the true Emmanuel, the "God with us" (Matthew 1:23). [12]

---

[12] Fr. Stephano Manelli, O.F.M., *The Most Blessed Sacrament: Our Lord is truly present: Body, Soul and Divinity to make you happy now and for all Eternity!*, Fr. Stephano Manelli, O.F.M., Imprimatur:

Or the following statement that defies any biblical basis:

> With Communion, Jesus enters my heart and re-
> mains corporally present in me as long as the spe-
> cies (the appearance: of bread) lasts; that is, for
> about 15 minutes. During this time, the Holy Fa-
> thers teach that the angels surround me to continue
> to adore Jesus and love Him without interruption.
> "When Jesus is corporally present within us, the
> angels surround us as a guard of love," wrote St.
> Bernard. [13]

Or a third statement that seems to reflect there is a
strong spiritual experience that acts as a powerful attrac-
tion to the Eucharistic Christ:

> All the saints have understood by experience the
> Divine marvel of the meeting and the union with
> Jesus in the Eucharist. They have understood that a
> devout Holy Communion means to be possessed
> by Him and to possess Him. One time St. Gemma
> Galgani wrote, "It is now night, tomorrow morning
> is approaching and then Jesus will possess me and
> I will possess Jesus." It is not possible to have a
> union more profound and more total: He in Me
> and I in Him; the one in the other. What more
> could we want?

New Focus on the Eucharist

Catholic Herald reporter Russell Shaw wrote an article
titled "New Focus on the Eucharist" that was posted on
the Internet October 2, 2003. In this article, he summarized

Antonius Zama, vic. generalis Neapoli, die 21, Aprilis 1973,
Children of the Father Foundation, Havertown, PA, page 4.
[13] Ibid.

the various events being promoted by Pope John Paul and then asked a very important question:

> Pope John Paul and the Vatican lately have been devoting more than ordinary high-level attention to the Eucharist, and now they apparently mean to devote even more. That raises an obvious question: Why?
>
> One clear signal was the encyclical, "Ecclesia de Eucharistia — On the Eucharist and its relationship to the Church," which John Paul published last Holy Thursday. The 14,500 word encyclical, the 14th issued by the pope, combines doctrine, admonition and testimony of faith in a distinctive, highly personal way.
>
> Then there is the apparent likelihood that the next general assembly of the world Synod of Bishops, which will probably take place next year or early 2005, will be on the Eucharist. If so, that means another papal document on that theme a year or two after the meeting.
>
> Considering all the issues clamoring for the attention of the pope, this is a remarkable amount of time and energy to invest in talking about the Blessed Sacrament. What is the reason? [14]

Two very interesting statements found on another web site called "Apostolate for Perpetual Eucharistic Adoration" seem to answer the question asked by Russell Shaw. Described as the "North American Apostolate of the Missionaries of the Blessed Sacrament, this group further de-

---

[14] Russell Shaw, "New Focus on the Eucharist," Online posting: www.catholicherald.com, cited October 2, 2003.

fines the goals of the New Evangelization program sanctioned by the Roman Catholic Church:

> The regular practice of Eucharistic adoration, which perpetual adoration fosters, must be at the root of the response. It enables us to respond to the Holy Father's call with "generosity and holiness." It fills our hearts with "new attitudes of humility, generosity and openness to purifying grace." It will prepare us for the "new evangelization" which will help restore all things in Christ.
>
> In his encyclical letter on the Eucharist, Domincae cenae, Pope John Paul said: "May our adoration never cease." That is what perpetual adoration is: adoration that never ceases. So let us continue to work hard for the spread of perpetual adoration so that our Holy Father's wish for perpetual adoration in every parish in the world may be fulfilled and that Christians of this millennium may witness the triumph of the Immaculate Heart of Mary and the Eucharistic Reign of Christ. [15]

Is it possible the New Evangelization program will use Eucharistic adoration to rekindle Eucharistic amazement and more and more people will be drawn by experience to the Eucharistic Christ? It is a fact that "Christianity" based on experience that is not supported biblically is one of the most effective ways to lead people astray. If the New Evangelization points people to the Eucharistic Christ that is associated with profound experiences that include healings, miracles and signs and wonders, will this have the potential to deceive?

---

[15] Online posting: www.perpetualadoration.org/ws200.htm, cited April 27, 2004.

In this chapter we have been looking at the New Evangelization program sanctioned by the Catholic Church for the third millennium. In the next chapter we will look at one of the methods endorsed by the Catholic Church that promotes an "amazement" centered on the Eucharistic Christ and Eucharistic adoration.

Chapter Seven
Adoring the Eucharist

Not long ago, as I was flipping through the channels on cable TV, I came across a program where a lady was giving her testimony. She said that although she had been a skeptic of psychic phenomena and the occult for many years, one day she decided to doubt her doubts and give the psychic realm a try. After repeating a mantra over and over again, she noticed that her personality began to change. Soon she was transferred to another level of consciousness. Her whole worldview was different from then on.

Isn't it interesting how people can be drawn into a belief system based on an experience that convinces them they have found the truth?

While visiting upstate New York, a friend of mine traveled with me to the Mormon tourist information center at the base of Hill Cumorah. We were soon surrounded by a number of Mormon missionaries who were more than willing to tell us about their faith. When I asked them how they knew Mormonism was true and that they were not being deceived, they gave me an answer based upon their experience.

The missionaries said they knew that what they believed was from God because they had received the "testimony." When I asked what they meant by "having received the testimony" they explained that they had experienced "the burning in the bosom." When I asked them where in the Bible the burning in the bosom could be found, they told me that not everything that God does is in the Bible.

On several occasions I have asked Mormons to give me more detailed information about this experience. All I have ever been told is that I should pray and ask God to give me a "burning-in-the-bosom" experience that would verify Mormonism is true. It seems that this experience is very important to Mormons. Once you have had this experience, and it seems to be a genuine experience, it is very difficult to convince a Mormon that their "restored gospel" is not the true gospel of Jesus Christ.

In this chapter we want to discuss a particular practice endorsed by the Catholic Church that promotes an experience-based Christianity that focuses on having a personal experience with the Eucharistic Christ. I will present the facts based on current events and then look to the Scriptures for insight and understanding.

What Is Eucharistic Adoration?

Up until now, we have been dealing primarily with the Catholic belief in transubstantiation and the belief in the "real presence of Jesus Christ." The Host, contained in a monstrance, is claimed to materialize into Jesus during Mass through the power of consecration.

But there is another aspect of the Eucharistic Christ that needs to be investigated. This is a teaching promoted by the Catholic Church that calls for adoration of the Eucharistic Christ while "He" is contained within the monstrance. In order to verify this belief we will examine several Catholic sources.

There are numerous web sites that specifically support Eucharistic adoration. In order to more clearly define what it means to be an "adorer of the Eucharist" I will quote one of these sites. Regarding transubstantiation we read:

Catholics believe that during Mass which we attend each week (for some of us daily), the priest (during the consecration) speaks these words as he holds the communion host, "*He took bread and gave thanks. He broke the bread, gave it to his disciples and said: Take this all of you, and eat it: this is my body which will be given up for you.*" When the priest says "this is my body" it is at that instant when, through the miracle of transubstantiation, the bread and the wine we offer as the bloodless sacrifice to our Lord truly become the Body, Blood, Soul and Divinity of Jesus. It is His true Presence in the form of bread and wine. It is Christ. [1]

Second, providing details regarding a practice called Perpetual Adoration, the web site claims:

Perpetual Adoration is when the priest takes a consecrated host, such as the one described above, and places it in a monstrance (monstrance comes from the Latin "monstrare" to show, to expose, to view). The monstrance is then placed in front of the tabernacle (an ornate box which holds the monstrance and any consecrated hosts) or on the altar of the church or chapel for adoration. [2]

Third, with reference to why Perpetual Adoration is so important, an additional statement is made:

---

[1] "What is Eucharistic Adoration?" online posting: www.medjugorje.org/adore.htm, cited February 1, 2004.
[2] Ibid.

What do you actually do during adoration? You may sign up to be an "adorer" which allows you to schedule yourself for one or more hours per week to pray before the very presence of Our Lord, exposed in the monstrance. It means that you can have some time alone with Jesus, to recite your favorite prayers, read the Bible, contemplate acts of faith, hope, charity, thanksgiving, reparation, pray a rosary or do whatever type of prayerful devotion that suits you before Our Lord. You can just sit and say nothing simply keeping Him company, just as you would with a dear friend. [3]

The Pope and Eucharistic Adoration

It is possible that after you have read the three previous quotes, a question comes to your mind. Is this really what Catholics are taught to believe, or is this just some fringe idea being promoted on an Internet web site that has no authority in representing what the Vatican endorses? Obviously that is a legitimate question. In order to answer this question, let's look at a statement made by the pope.

I came across this statement in the *Zenit* April 17, 2003 article that was quoted earlier in chapter 6, regarding Pope John Paul's call to "rekindle Eucharistic amazement." [4] At the very end of that article, the pope was quoted as saying:

...(although) the liturgical reform inaugurated by the [Second Vatican] Council has greatly contributed to a more conscious, active, fruitful participation in the Holy Sacrifice of the Altar on the part of the faithful (unfortunately) alongside these lights,

---

[3] Ibid.
[4] "Why the Pope would Write and Encyclical on the Eucharist: To Rekindle Amazement," *Zenit: The World Seen From Rome,* cited April 17, 2003, online posting: www.zenit.org/english.

there are also shadows. In fact there are places where there is almost total abandonment of the practice of Eucharistic adoration. [5]

While it is obvious the pope was encouraged by what he called the "fruitful participation in the Holy Sacrifice of the Altar on the part of the faithful," he also had some concerns. As he stated: "there are places where there is almost total abandonment of the practice of Eucharistic adoration."

It is apparent that if this "abandonment" of Eucharistic adoration has produced what he calls "shadows," he must be in favor of the practice.

The fact that the pope is an advocate of Eucharistic adoration can be documented from various sources. For example, in a message delivered by Pope John Paul II on the topic of Perpetual Adoration of the Eucharist delivered at the Forty-fifth International Eucharistic Congress, Seville, Spain, June 1993, he said:

> Beloved priests, religious men and religious women, most beloved brothers and sisters, it is for me a motive of special joy to prostrate myself with you before Jesus in the Blessed Sacrament in an act of humble adoration, of praise to the merciful God, of thanksgiving to the Giver of all that is good, of supplication to Him whom is always alive to intercede for us.

> Perpetual Adoration of Jesus in the Blessed Sacrament has been a connecting thread of all the acts of this International Eucharistic Congress. I hope that this form of Adoration, with permanent exposition of the Blessed Sacrament, will continue into the

---

[5] Ibid.

future. Specifically, I hope that the fruit of this Congress results in the establishment of Perpetual Adoration in all parishes and Christian communities throughout the world. [6]

The Catholic Catechism and Eucharistic Adoration

When not certain what the Catholic Church really teaches, it is always important to turn to the *Catechism of the Catholic Church*. In the introduction, Pope John Paul II endorses this document as a true source of Catholic doctrine. In a statement given October 11, 1992 at the opening of the Second Vatican Ecumenical Council, the pope endorsed the *Catechism of the Catholic Church* the following way:

> The *Catechism of the Catholic Church,* which I approved June 25th last and the publication of which I today order by virtue of my Apostolic Authority, is a statement of the Church's faith and of catholic doctrine, attested to or illuminated by Sacred Scripture, the Apostolic Tradition and the Church's Magisterium. I declare it to be a sure norm for teaching the faith and thus a valid and legitimate instrument for ecclesial communion. May it serve the renewal to which the Holy Spirit ceaselessly calls the Church of God, the Body of Christ, on her pilgrimage to the undiminished light of the Kingdom! [7]

---

[6] "Pope on Exposition of the Blessed Sacrament," cited February 20, 2004, online posting:
www.blessedsacrament.com/theology/q173.html.
[7] Pope John Paul II, "Introduction," *Catechism of the Catholic Church,* An Image Book, Doubleday, New York, 1994, page 5.

In order to substantiate what the *Catechism of the Catholic Church* states about this topic of Eucharistic adoration, the following items are quoted:

> 1183 The *tabernacle* is to be situated "in churches in a most worthy place with the greatest of honor" (Paul VI, *Mysterium Fidei:* AAS (1965) 771). The dignity, the placing and the security of the Eucharistic tabernacle should foster adoration before the Lord really present in the Blessed Sacrament of the altar. [8]

> 1378 *Worship of the Eucharist.* In the liturgy of the Mass we express our faith in the real presence of Christ under the species of bread and wine by, among other ways, genuflecting or bowing deeply as a sign of adoration of the Lord. "The Catholic Church has always offered and still offers to the sacrament of the Eucharist the cult of adoration, not only during Mass, but also outside of it, reserving the consecrated hosts with the utmost care, exposing them to the solemn veneration of the faithful, and carrying them in procession" (Paul VI, *MF* 46). [9]

> 1379 The tabernacle was first intended for the reservation of the Eucharist in a worthy place so that it could be brought to the sick and those absent, outside of Mass. As faith in the real presence of Christ in his Eucharist deepened, the Church became conscious of the meaning of silent adoration of the Lord present under the Eucharistic species. It is for this reason that the tabernacle should be located in an especially worthy place in the church

---

[8] Ibid., page 306.
[9] Ibid., page 347.

and should be constructed in such a way that it emphasizes and manifests the truth of the real presence of Christ in the Blessed Sacrament. [10]

1380 It is highly fitting that Christ should have wanted to remain present in the Church in this unique way. Since Christ was about to take his departure from his own visible form, he wanted to give us his sacramental presence; since he was about to offer himself on the cross to save us, he wanted us to have the memorial of the love with which he loved us "to the end" (*Jn* 13:1), even to the giving of his life. In his Eucharistic presence he remains mysteriously in our midst as the one who loved us and gave himself up for us (*Gal.* 2:20) and he remains under signs that express and communicate this love:

> The Church and the world have a great need for Eucharistic worship. Jesus awaits us in this sacrament of love. Let us not refuse the time to go and meet him in adoration, in contemplation full of faith, and open to making amends for the serious offenses and crimes of the world. Let our adoration never cease   (John Paul II, *Dominicae cenae* 3). [11]

Numerous other references regarding Eucharistic adoration from the *Catechism of the Catholic Church* could also be cited. However with what has already been quoted, the point should be clear. Eucharistic adoration is not an insignificant idea manufactured by a fringe group of experiential fanatics. The practice is firmly endorsed by the pope

---

[10] Ibid., page 348.
[11] Ibid. page 348.

and is a fundamental necessity for all those who call the Catholic Church their church.

Putting the Practice into Practice

One of the reasons for writing this book is to inform people about a current trend that is underway and to warn about the potential for a coming great delusion in the name of Christ that the Bible clearly teaches will happen. On occasion when I have talked about some of the things that have been mentioned in this book to other Bible-believing Christians, I have been met with an attitude of indifference. "Why would you waste your time in talking about this?" one pastor asked me. "This isn't an important topic. Even Catholics don't believe in such foolishness anymore."

Comments like these, I have found to be quite discouraging. When people are warned about what is happening, they often don't want to hear. Or even if they hear, many do not care. "Why can't we just agree to disagree?" several Christian leaders have told me. But the fact these things are happening and that they are supported by the authority of the Catholic Church compel me to sound the alarm.

In the case of Eucharistic adoration, it would be good to examine the facts. The magnitude of the movement promoting Eucharistic adoration is staggering. While not new, as I have already pointed out, it is becoming increasingly more popular and widespread.

For example, if you have access to the Internet, check out a web site called "The Real Presence Association" located at www.therealpresence.org/index.html. There on the home page you will see an opened gate with three phrases that alternately become visible: "Leave the Darkness," "Come into the Light," and "Visit the Lord." An additional click of the mouse on the directory will open another page that shows a map of the United States with the heading "Churches and Chapels that have Eucharistic Adoration" and the following statement: "To locate an adoration site nearest you, click a state on the map above or on one of the links below, then search by city." Click on any state (or all of the states). You will see thousands of churches, locations of the churches and the specific times for Eucharistic adoration listed.

If you are still not convinced this phenomenon is actually happening, do a search on the Internet on the topic of Eucharistic adoration. I am certain this exercise will open your eyes to the fact that there is a global agenda to promote Eucharistic adoration thus fulfilling the challenge John Paul II gave at the Eucharistic Congress, in Seville, in 1993:

> Perpetual Adoration of Jesus in the Blessed Sacrament has been a connecting thread of all the acts of this International Eucharistic Congress. I hope that this form of Adoration, with permanent exposition of the Blessed Sacrament, will continue into the future. Specifically, I hope that the fruit of this Congress results in the establishment of Perpetual Adoration in all parishes and Christian communities throughout the world. [12]

Seeing Is Believing

One might still wonder—do people really believe in Eucharistic adoration or is this just another teaching of the Catholic Church that no one really follows? In the fall of 2003, a pastor friend of mine and I visited St Patrick's Cathedral in the city of New York. As I had already checked "The Real Presence" web site, I knew when to go and what we would see.

---

[12] "Pope on Exposition of the Blessed Sacrament."

Behind the main altar where Mass is performed, there was an area where people were kneeling and praying before a monstrance. Behind this monstrance that contained a consecrated Host, there was a very large statue of Mary. Several custodians were watching over the area making sure that the adorers would be permitted to adore in silence.

Another example of Eucharistic adoration in action can be demonstrated by visiting a web site called "Visit the Savior" at www.savior.org. On the home page you will read the following statement:

> Savior.org's mission is that of increasing awareness and devotion to our Lord in the Most Blessed Sacrament. We also seek to bring the live image of His living Presence to the homebound, the workplace, and to remote areas around the world.[13]

Several testimonies are available at this site given by individuals who have visited the site. A web camera is focused on a monstrance containing a consecrated Host, twenty-four hours a day, every day. Visitors to the site are encouraged to adore "Jesus" on-line. A testimony posted from Cindy from Alabama states:

> I know that this will sound crazy, but I guess I should start from the beginning. Tonight was the first time I prayed my rosary in front of Jesus on-line. Right after I finished saying the rosary. I saw a distinct face. I can still see his eyes, crown of thorns, nose and beard. I cannot explain it, but I guess he must be very pleased with your work. I am not crazy. I do go adore Jesus in the Blessed Sacrament in person where I live, but just wanted

---

[13] Visit the Savior Home page, cited December 2003, online posting: www.savior.org.

to pray in front of him at home tonight on your site rather than not adoring him at all. When I came to write to you I still saw his face. I will be telling many other people about what a blessing your site is to all around the world. [14]

Idolatry

Previously, in chapter 4, we have demonstrated from the Scriptures that the Eucharistic Jesus is not the Jesus of the Bible. Therefore, the Eucharistic Christ must be a false christ. To worship or adore anyone or anything other than the true and living God is called idolatry in the Bible. The Creator alone deserves all our worship, not any created thing.

How serious is idolatry? Let's review several Scripture passages, starting with the second commandment:

You shall not make for yourself a carved image, or any likeness of anything that is in heaven above, or that is in the earth beneath, or that is in the water under the earth; **you shall not bow down to them nor serve them**. For I, the LORD your God, am a jealous God. [15]

Cursed is the one who makes a carved or molded image, an abomination to the LORD, the work of the hands of the craftsman... [16]

Do you not know that the unrighteous will not inherit the kingdom of God? Do not be deceived. Neither fornicators, **nor idolaters**, nor adulterers, nor homosexuals, nor sodomites, nor thieves, nor

---

[14] Ibid.
[15] Exodus 20:4-5
[16] Deuteronomy 27:15

covetous, nor drunkards, nor revilers, nor extortioners will inherit the kingdom of God. [17]

But the rest of mankind, who were not killed by these plagues, did not repent of the works of their hands, that they should not worship demons, and idols of gold, silver, brass, stone, and wood, which can neither see nor hear nor walk. [18]

It is very apparent that God abhors idolatry and that worshipping anyone else or anything or any image has grave eternal consequences.

Gathering the Data

By now, if you have read through the previous chapters, a picture should be shaping in your mind. A quick overview of what we have already covered will perhaps make that picture clearer.

It is a fact that the pope has called the Catholic Church to a missionary vision centered on pointing people to the Eucharistic Jesus. This Eucharistic Jesus, according to Catholic dogma, can be manifested on the altar of a Catholic Church and be placed on display in a container. It is also a fact the Catholic Church believes that adoring the "Eucharistic Christ" is an act of worship that can result in a profound experience with which all Catholics should become familiar.

But it is also a fact that the Bible teaches adoring graven images that are created to supposedly represent God, are an abomination unto God. Therefore, if this practice of Eucharistic adoration is merely a practice based on tradition and without a scriptural precedence, it would also follow that God must look upon this practice as deceptive and

---

[17] 1 Corinthians 6:9-10
[18] Revelation 9:20

wrong. Additionally, for someone or some group to accept something that is wrong as something that is from God would require a spiritual delusion authored by a spiritual deceiver.

Finally, if the Bible teaches there is a spiritual deceiver who has an agenda to deceive in the name of Christ, and that there will be a time when there will be false appearances of Christ associated with lying signs and wonders, is it not reasonable to warn people when we see this happening?

In the next chapter we will examine signs and wonders associated with the Eucharistic Christ.

Chapter Eight
Eucharistic Miracles

Signs and wonders! The very mention of the miraculous causes the average person to pay attention.

Human beings are designed to live in a physical world that we perceive by our senses. We gather information that comes to our brains from what we see, feel, touch, taste and smell. However, there is also a spiritual dimension that exists beyond the material dimension.

When we consider the area of signs and wonders, we are dealing with phenomena that occur at the interface of the natural and the spiritual dimensions. Since Satan's appearance to Eve in the Garden of Eden, our planet has been engaged in a constant battle that involves combat between the spiritual and natural realms. Because there are two sides to the spiritual dimension, holy and unholy, it is obvious that not everything that originates from the spiritual realm necessarily comes from God.

The apostle Paul warned the church at Ephesus about this very matter. He wrote:

Put on the whole armor of God, that you may be able to stand against the wiles of the devil. For we do not wrestle against flesh and blood, but against principalities, against powers, against the rulers of the darkness of this age, against spiritual hosts of wickedness in the heavenly places. [1]

While the Bible teaches that God is a God who performs signs, wonders and miracles, we are also warned there is a spiritual dimension that can be deceptive and lead people astray. In fact, one of the signs of the last times according to Jesus, would be the fact that this period of time would be characterized by great deception involving "lying signs and wonders." As Jesus stated:

Then if anyone says to you, "Look, here is the Christ!" or "There!" do not believe it. For false christs and false prophets will rise and show great signs and wonders to deceive, if possible, even the elect. [2]

Not long after my first book on experience-based Christianity was published, *New Wine or Old Deception,* I received a phone call from an elderly lady who was not pleased by the contents of the book. As she lived in the same area, I agreed to meet with her and discuss her concerns. I discovered she was upset because of statements that had been made in the book warning people about the potential danger of signs and wonders and the role they played in deceiving people in the last days. She was convinced that the Bible taught that Jesus could not return until there was a great revival and the whole world came to Jesus through signs and wonders.

Unfortunately, this view is accepted by a vast number of professing Christians. In fact it is becoming more and more apparent the world is being prepared and conditioned to accept "lying signs and wonders" that set up the

---

[1] Ephesians 6:11-12
[2] Matthew 24:23-24

world for the deception Jesus warned would take place in His name.

This chapter is about signs and wonders that are associated with the Eucharistic Christ. Although Eucharistic miracles have been commonplace in the past, current trends indicate this phenomenon is on the upswing.

What is a Eucharistic Miracle?

I came across the term *Eucharistic miracle* for the first time when I was reading a booklet about messages that had been received from an apparition claiming to be Mary, the mother of Jesus. These messages were supposedly revealed to a woman by the name of Ida Peerdeman from the city of Amsterdam. The first message that Peerdeman claimed she received occurred on March 25, 1945. [3]

In the introduction of the booklet there was a statement that mentioned that 600 years previous to Peerdeman's visitation, an event took place in Amsterdam that became known as the "Miracle of Amsterdam." This so-called miracle was associated with the Eucharist. According to the booklet:

> The miracle occurred when the priest was called to administer last rites to a sick and dying man. After confession he received Holy Communion, but soon afterward he had to vomit. The woman nursing him swept it all up including the vomited host and threw it into the fire in the hearth. The host, however, remained floating above the flames. It was taken and kept in a linen chest for some time and then silently brought to the church. But the next day it was found back in the chest. The occurrence

---

[3] *The Daily Miracle: The Eucharistic Experiences*, (A summary), The Netherlands, 1999, page 7.

repeated itself twice. Finally, the ecclesiastical authorities understood that the miracle should be made public and they decided to have the host brought to the church in solemn procession. Following official investigations, the bishop of Utrecht permitted the proclamation of the miracle in 1346. Thus the High Feast of the Blessed Sacrament came into being and many pilgrims came to Amsterdam. [4]

This first encounter with the "Miracle of Amsterdam" triggered my interest to do more research. I discovered a book titled *Eucharistic Miracles: And Eucharistic Phenomena in the Lives of the Saints*, authored by Joan Carroll Cruz. It was this book that showed me that the "Miracle of Amsterdam" was merely the tip of the iceberg.

The back cover of Cruz's book gave an overview of the content. We read:

On numerous occasions in the history of the Church, God has seen fit to offer miraculous visible proof of the Catholic teaching that at the sacred words of Consecration of the Mass, the bread and wine upon the altar are truly changed into the Body and Blood of Jesus Christ. Joan Carroll Cruz's *Eucharistic Miracles* recounts 36 such major Eucharistic miracles in Church history. She tells of Hosts which have turned to visible flesh, Hosts that have bled, Hosts which have become hard as flint when received by a person in mortal sin, Hosts that have levitated, Hosts which have manifested their hidden presence by mysterious lights, consecrated "wine" which turned into visible blood etc., as well as many miracles which occurred after sacrilege

---

4 Ibid.

had been committed against the Holy Eucharist. The events told here cover a wide historical gamut, the first miracle described being that of Lanciano, Italy in the 8th century and the last in Stich, Bavaria in 1970. [5]

As stated, the book presented a chronological account from the eighth century to the present regarding alleged miraculous occurrences associated with the Eucharist. However, nowhere in the book is the Bible used to substantiate these miracles. Cruz claimed that her purpose in writing the book was to impress the readers about the importance of believing in transubstantiation. In the introduction she writes:

> The greatest treasure in the Catholic Church is, without question, the Holy Eucharist — in which Jesus Christ humbly assumes the appearance of bread. Whether retained in simple chapels or grand basilicas, the Eucharist remains a sign of the Heavenly Father's unwillingness to be physically separated from His children.

> His children on the other hand, have not always appreciated this presence and, as painful as it is to consider, many have abused the gift by receiving it unworthily, by doubting the Real Presence of God in the sacred Host, or by treating the Sacrament with indifference. For these reasons the Savior has seen fit at times to prove His presence by performing Eucharistic miracles of various kinds. [6]

---

[5] Joan Carroll Cruz, *Eucharistic Miracles*, Tan Books and Publishers, Rockford, IL, 1987, page xiii, Imprimatur, Phillip M. Hannan, Archbishop of New Orleans, April 25, 1986, back cover.

[6] Ibid., page xi.

This brings up an interesting point. If the "Savior" is actually the reason for these Eucharistic miracles, is there a documented record to show that Eucharistic miracles actually have been instrumental in helping people understand the gospel of the true Savior, Jesus Christ? Or were these people only impressed to believe in the Real Presence in a wafer, which is a foundation of the Roman Catholic Church?

Historical Consequences of Denying Transubstantiation

It is also important to mention not everyone agrees that the Eucharistic miracles that occurred in the past were from God. For example, J. C. Ryle writing about the history of the Eucharist from another perspective, explains what happened when people refused to accept the Roman Catholic belief in the Real Presence:

> The point I refer to is the special reason why our reformers were burned. Great indeed would be our mistake if we supposed that they suffered in the vague charge of refusing submission to the Pope, or desiring to maintain the independence of the Church of England. Nothing of the kind! The principal reason why they were burned was because they refused one of the peculiar doctrines of the Romish church. On that doctrine, in almost every case, hinged their life or death. If they admitted it, they might live, if they refused it, they must die. The doctrine in question was the real presence of the body and blood of Christ in the consecrated elements of bread and wine in the Lord's Supper. [7]

---

[7] J. C. Ryle, *Light from Old Times - Volume 1*, Charles Nolan Publishers, Moscow, ID, 1890, pages 54-55.

Or consider the following quotation taken from *Foxe's Book of Martyrs*. Mrs. Prest of Cornwall was accused of denying transubstantiation by Catholic authorities. Her final words to the Catholic bishop prior to being burned at the stake are very illuminating:

[Can you] deny your creed which says that Christ doth perpetually sit at the right hand of His Father, both body and soul, until He comes again; or whether He be there in heaven our Advocate, and to make prayer for us unto God His Father? If He be so, He is not here on earth in a piece of bread. If He be not here, and if He do not dwell in temples made with hands, but in heaven, what! Shall we seek Him here? If He did not offer His body once for all, why make you a new offering? If with one offering He made all perfect, why do you with a false offering make all imperfect? If He be to be worshipped in spirit and in truth, why do you worship a piece of bread? If He be eaten and drunken in faith and truth, if His flesh is not profitable to be among us, why do you say you make His flesh and blood, and say it is profitable for body and soul? Alas! I am a poor woman, but rather than to do as you do, I would live no longer. [8]

Can History be Repeated?

Since we live in the here and now, we are limited to what we know by what is observed in the present. However, if we make the effort to investigate what has happened in the past, we would find out that understanding the past is often a key to understanding the present. This is

---

[8] John Foxe, *Foxe's Book of Martyrs*, Nashville, Tennessee, Thomas Nelson Publishers, 2000, page 155.

especially true when we examine the past and the present from a spiritual perspective.

Solomon made this point clear in the Book of Ecclesiastes. He wrote:

> That which has been is what will be, that which is done is what will be done, and there is nothing new under the sun. Is there anything of which it may be said, "See, this is new"? It has already been in ancient times before us. There is no remembrance of former things, nor will there be any remembrance of things that are to come by those who will come after. [9]

This biblical principle is particularly important in our study of Eucharistic miracles. Could Eucharistic miracles be the cause for mass conversions into Roman Catholicism in the future? If people died for standing up against transubstantiation in the past, is it possible that this could happen again?

Current trends indicate that Eucharistic miracles are on the upswing. For example, Michael Brown, in his book *Secrets of the Eucharist*, gives an account of what he believes is a modern day example in the following quote:

> Incredibly, Eucharistic miracles are such today that there will soon be too many to recount. As with anything we must await verification. And whatever we may feel, we must be obedient to the local Bishop. Let me give one recent example. In February of 1996, at the Mission Church of Holy Family in Barbeau, Michigan, it was reported that a consecrated Host in an ablution cup next to the tabernacle began to change color. It had been placed there

---

[9] Ecclesiastes 1:9-11

for dissolution because a Eucharistic minister had dropped it during Mass, but instead of dissolving in water, strange things began to happen. A week after it was first placed in the cup, the Host appeared to be turning red. There was a dime-sized spot on the Host. Soon it grew and darkened.

While the Bishop worried that it might be a simple case of fungus (which has happened in some cases), the Host was soon engulfed in "blood-red liquid which prevented us from seeing much detail. The dish was completely crimson red," claimed Father McQuesten. Within three weeks the Host's appearance was "fleshlike," according to the priest. It looked like a gleaming red heart with darker red in the middle. [10]

A second reference regarding a recent Eucharistic miracle is taken from a letter sent by Bishop Claudio Gatti on 15th of June 2000, to cardinals, bishops and priests. According to Bishop Gatti, he too experienced a modern day Eucharistic miracle:

On the 11th of June 2000, feast of Pentecost, while I was celebrating Holy Mass in the church "Mother of the Eucharist," a great Eucharistic miracle happened. As soon as I finished saying the wording of the consecration of bread, blood began to come out from my host. Time stopped for me. I was bending over the host that I was holding tightly in my

---

[10] Michael H. Brown, *Secrets of the Eucharist*, Queenship Publishing Company, Goleta, CA, 1996, page 37.

hands and was gazing at the divine blood that was spreading on a great part of its surface. [11]

Third, a testimony given by Father Johnson Karoor, a Catholic priest in India, shows that these Eucharistic miracles are happening all around the world:

> On the 28th April 2001, we held the novena prayer to St. Jude in the parish church at Chirattakonam as usual. At about 8:49 a.m. I exposed the Holy Eucharist in the monstrance and we started the adoration. During the adoration I saw three dots on the holy Eucharist. I stopped reciting the prayers and as if from some sort of an inner inspiration I just stood looking at the Eucharist. As the novena prayer was over I gave the faithful Eucharistic benediction. Then I invited the attention of the Faithful to the monstrance and they testified that they saw three dots on the Eucharist. I asked the faithful to remain in prayer and I kept the Holy Eucharist in the tabernacle.
>
> I celebrated the Holy Mass on Monday, the 30th April and on the next day I left for Trivandrum. After returning from Trivandrum on Saturday Morning 5th May 2001, I opened the church for the liturgical service. I vested myself and opened the tabernacle. Immediately I noticed the figure of a human face in yellow color in the Eucharist. I was at a loss what to do. I just stood there for a few seconds. I asked the faithful to kneel down and pray. I thought it was something which I alone experienced. I kept the holy Eucharist in the monstrance

---

[11] Bishop Claudio Gatti, Letter, June 15, 2000, online posting: www.madredelleucaristia.it/eng/letters5.htm, cited December 3, 2003.

and asked the mass server whether he saw something in the Eucharist. "I see a figure", he said. I saw the faithful looking intently at the monstrance observing the figure. We started the adoration. During the adoration we saw the figure becoming clearer. I didn't have the strength to speak anything to the faithful. I stood aside for sometime. I couldn't control my tears. [12]

More Appearances

The more I researched and read, the more I realized there is an obvious pattern being established. Reported Eucharistic miracles are becoming more convincing to those who witness these events. In fact, faces of "Jesus" associated with the consecrated Host are being reported in many different places.

A statement that Michael Brown makes in his book, *Secrets of the Eucharist*, may give insight into where this trend is leading. He states:

Only a priest can consecrate. The consecrated hands are of overwhelming and yet little appreciated importance. When the Host is held aloft, you can nearly feel the presence of those many saints and angels. You can nearly see Christ's Face in the large wafer. There is a hush and also a sense of tranquility. The Prince of Peace has arrived. He has entered. He is with us. [13]

Based on the current trends that have been brought to our attention it is becoming more and more obvious that

---

[12] Testimony of the parish priest Fr. Johnson Karoor, online posting: http://malankara.net/eucharist/eucharist.htm, cited July 10, 2003.
[13] Michael H. Brown, page 19.

something very significant is about to happen. The pope's call for a missionary vision centered on the Eucharist enhanced by Eucharistic adoration appears to be having results.

What if apparitions of the Eucharistic Christ become increasingly more frequent in Roman Catholic Churches? What if people from other faiths were to hear about these apparitions and then begin to experience them for themselves? What if signs and wonders including miraculous healings started to happen? What if these appearances were so powerful that Muslims, Hindus, Protestants, and even skeptics were converted?

Corruption

Before leaving this chapter, those familiar with God's Word may have noticed another major unbiblical aspect of the Eucharist. Even proponents of transubstantiation will acknowledge that the consecrated wafer (the real presence of Jesus) has been known to become moldy, corrupted, and rot if not ingested in a reasonable time. Of course, if the consecrated elements were truly Jesus' body, this would be impossible. Repeatedly the Bible states that Jesus' body would NOT experience corruption. The apostle Peter, quoting from David in the 16th Psalm, explains this in the Book of Acts:

> For You [God the Father] will not leave my soul in Hades, **Nor will You allow Your Holy One [Jesus Christ] to see corruption.**..."Men and brethren, let me speak freely to you of the patriarch David, that he is both dead and buried, and his tomb is with us to this day. "Therefore, being a prophet, and knowing that God had sworn with an oath to him that of the fruit of his body, according to the flesh, He would raise up the Christ to sit on his throne, **"he, foreseeing this, spoke concerning the resur-**

rection of the Christ, that His soul was not left in Hades, nor did His flesh see corruption. [14]

In the next chapter we will continue presenting a scenario that shows how the world is being prepared for an experienced-based Christianity founded on lying signs and wonders that has the potential for uniting together the religions of the world for the cause of peace.

---

[14] Acts 2:27, 29-31

Chapter Nine
Eucharistic Conversions

According to the Catholic Catechism, the Eucharist is the sum and summary of the Catholic faith. [1] In order to become a Roman Catholic, a person must accept that Jesus Christ truly is present in the consecrated Host.

Throughout this book we have been examining the importance of the Eucharist to the Roman Catholic faith. First, we documented that Pope John Paul II called for a missionary vision for the Roman Catholic Church to be centered on the Eucharist. Second, we saw how the pope followed up this vision by challenging the faithful to "rekindle amazement" in the Eucharist through the practice of Eucharistic adoration.

Further, evidence was presented to show that this "rekindling" of amazement for the Eucharist has been having a major impact. Not only did we see that active programs for adoring the Host are underway worldwide, but there are also a number of testimonies made by adorers of the Eucharist showing that Eucharistic miracles are impacting Catholics.

---

[1] *Catechism of the Catholic Church*, An Image Book, Doubleday, New York, 1994, page 334.

While these miracles seem to build up the faith of the faithful and make Catholics better Catholics, a question needs to be asked. What role is the Eucharist having as an evangelistic tool that is influencing those who are not Roman Catholic? In other words, is there any evidence to show the New Evangelization centered on the Eucharist and Eucharistic adoration is effective in bringing people to the Eucharistic Christ? Is the Eucharist proving to be an effective means in evangelizing non-Catholics into the Catholic faith?

This chapter will provide documentation to show that there is evidence that the New Evangelization centered on the Eucharist is gaining converts. We will present several testimonies from individuals who have converted to Catholicism—explaining how the Eucharist played a central role in their conversion process.

Peter Kreeft

Peter Kreeft, Ph.D., is a professor of philosophy at Boston College. He is a regular contributor to several Christian publications, is in wide demand as a speaker at conferences, and is the author of over forty books dealing with spirituality, apologetics and philosophy. [2] Dr. Kreeft, once a Dutch Reformed Protestant, converted to Roman Catholicism. He is considered by many to be a leader in the area of Christian apologetics, even by Protestants.

One of Peter Kreeft's books is *Ecumenical Jihad*. On the back cover of this book there are a number of endorsements by well-known evangelical leaders. For example:

> Peter Kreeft is one of the premier apologists in America today, witty, incisive and powerful. On

---

[2] Online posting: http://www.peterkreeft.com/about.htm, cited December 15, 2003.

the front lines in today's culture war, Kreeft is one of our most valiant intellectual warriors. —Chuck Colson [3]

This racy little book opens up a far-reaching theme. With entertaining insight, Kreeft looks into the attitudes, alliances and strategies that today's state of affairs requires of believers. Catholics, Protestants and Orthodox alike need to ponder Peter Kreeft's vision of things—preferably in discussion together. What if he is right?—J. I. Packer [4]

In order to understand Dr. Kreeft's spiritual journey it is helpful to examine a number of testimonial statements that he made in *Ecumenical Jihad*. For example, regarding the role that the Eucharist played in his conversion to Roman Catholicism, he wrote:

> In my conversion from Dutch Reformed Calvinism to Roman Catholicism, the one Catholic dogma that most drew me was the Eucharist. [5]

Now, as a strong promoter of the Roman Catholic Church, Kreeft believes that the teaching of transubstantiation and the "Real Presence of Christ" in the Eucharist has potential for winning other Protestants back to the "Mother of All Churches." Although he recognizes the Catholic Church's view on the Sacrament of the Eucharist was instrumental in bringing about division between Protestants and Catholics in the past, he believes there is potential for the Eucharist to now be an evangelistic tool to bring back the "separated brethren" to Roman Catholicism. As he stated in his book:

---

[3] Peter Kreeft, *Evangelical Jihad*, Ignatius Press, San Francisco, 1996, back cover, endorsement by Chuck Colson.
[4] Ibid., endorsement by J. I. Packer.
[5] Ibid., page 145.

No Catholic dogma is so distinctive and so apparently anti-ecumenical as the dogma of the Real Presence of Christ in the Eucharist. Yet this dogma may be the greatest cause of ecumenism and eventual reunion. [6]

Further, predicting that ecumenism for the future would be fostered by the very factors that once brought about division, Kreeft continued:

I found this doctrine, which seemed to repel and divide, at the same time attracted and united. The same with Mary: she—who is a point of division between Catholics and Protestants—she may bring the churches together again and heal the tears in her Son's visible body on earth, she, the very one who seems to divide Catholics from Protestants. The most distinctive Catholic doctrines, especially those concerning the Eucharist and Mary, may prove the most unifying and attracting ones. [7]

Finally, Peter Kreeft expresses his heartfelt concern for those Protestants who still refuse to accept the Catholic teaching of the Real Presence of Christ in a wafer. He wrote:

When I think how much my Protestant brothers and sisters are missing in not having Christ's Real Presence in the Eucharist; when I kneel before the Eucharist and realize I am as truly in Christ's presence as the apostles were but that my Protestant brothers and sisters don't know that, don't believe that—I at first feel a terrible gap between myself

---

[6] Ibid., page 145.
[7] Ibid., page 158.

and them. What a tremendous thing they are missing! [8]

Scott Hahn

Dr. Scott Hahn is a Professor of Theology and Scripture at Franciscan University of Steubenville, where he has taught since 1990. He is the founder and director of the Saint Paul Center for Biblical Theology.

Hahn entered the Catholic Church at Easter 1986. He is a former ordained Presbyterian minister with ten years of ministry experience in Protestant congregations and a former Professor of Theology at Chesapeake Theological Seminary. He received his Bachelor of Arts degree with a triple-major in Theology, Philosophy and Economics from Grove City College, Pennsylvania, in 1979; his Masters of Divinity from Gordon-Conwell Theological Seminary in 1982; and his Ph.D. in Biblical Theology from Marquette University in 1995.

An exceptionally popular speaker and teacher, Dr. Hahn has delivered numerous talks nationally and internationally on a wide variety of topics related to Scripture and the Catholic faith. His teaching has been effective in helping thousands of Protestants and fallen away Catholics to (re)embrace the Catholic faith. [9]

Both Scott and his wife Kimberly have written about their spiritual journey that brought them to the Roman Catholic Church in a book called *Rome Sweet Rome: Our*

---

[8] Ibid., page 159.
[9] Online posting: http://www.scotthahn.com/docview/view.phtml?doc=schedul e/vbio.phtml&rdoc=Hahn%20Speaking%20Event%20Informati on&return=/speaking.phtml, cited December 15, 2003.

Journey to Catholicism. [10] On the back cover of their book a statement is made that provides further information about the Hahn family:

> For the last decade, Scott and Kimberly Hahn have been speaking around the country—and making tapes that circulate the globe—sharing with thousands all about their conversion to the Catholic Church and the truth and splendor of the Catholic faith. Now this outstanding Catholic husband and wife have finally put their story into print as they recount their incredible spiritual journey "back home" into God's worldwide family, the Catholic Church. [11]

In *Rome Sweet Rome: Our Journey to Catholicism,* Scott Hahn gives us a step by step account of a Eucharistic encounter that was instrumental in his conversion to Roman Catholicism. Hahn describes in detail what happened to him one day when he attended a Catholic Mass. He wrote:

> The one day, I made a "fatal blunder"—I decided that it was time for me to go to Mass on my own. Finally, resolved to darken the doors of Gesu, Marquette University's parish. Right before noon, I slipped quietly into the basement of the chapel for daily Mass. I wasn't sure what to expect; maybe I'd be all alone with a priest and a couple of old nuns. I took a seat as an observer in the back pew.
>
> All of a sudden lots of ordinary people began coming in off the streets—rank-and-file type folks. They came in, genuflected, knelt and prayed. Their simple but sincere devotion was impressive.

---

[10] Scott and Kimberly Hahn, *Rome Sweet Rome: Our Journey to Catholicism,* Ignatius Press, San Francisco, 1993.
[11] Ibid., back cover.

Then a bell rang and a priest walked toward the altar. I remained seated; I wasn't sure if it was safe to kneel. As an evangelical Calvinist, I had been taught that the Catholic Mass was the greatest sacrilege that a man could commit — to resacrifice Christ — so I wasn't sure what to do. [12]

Hahn then described in detail the thoughts and feeling that overcame him as the priest proceeded with the consecration of the Host:

> After pronouncing the words of consecration, the priest held up the Host. I felt as if the last drop of doubt had drained from me. With all of my heart, I whispered, "My Lord and my God. That's really you! And if that's you, then I want full communion with you. I don't want to hold anything back."
>
> Then I remembered my promise: 1990. Oh yes, I've got to regain control — I'm a Presbyterian, right? And with that I left the chapel, not telling a soul where or what I had done. But the next day I was back, and the next and the next. Within a week or two I was hooked. I don't know how to say it, but I had fallen head over heels in love with our Lord in the Eucharist. His presence to me in the Blessed Sacrament was powerful and personal. As I sat in the back I began to kneel and pray with the others whom I now knew to be my brothers and sisters. I wasn't an orphan! I had found my family — it was God's family. [13]

Soon the conversion process was completed. Hahn was overcome by his experience and was convinced that he

---

[12] Ibid., page 87.
[13] Ibid.

truly had discovered the Real Presence of Christ in the Eucharist. In his own words:

> Day after day, witnessing the entire drama of the Mass, I saw the covenant renewed before my very eyes. I knew Christ wanted me to receive him by faith, not just spiritually in my heart, but physically as well: onto my tongue, down my throat and into my whole body and soul. This was what the Incarnation was all about. This was the gospel in its fullness.
>
> Each day after Mass, I spent a half hour to an hour praying the Rosary. I felt the Lord unleash his power through his Mother before the Blessed Sacrament. I begged him to open up my heart to show me his will. [14]

Kimberly Hahn

While Scott was converted in 1986, Kimberly's conversion did not happen until four years later. In one section of *Rome Sweet Rome: Our Journey to Catholicism*, Kimberly Hahn described the struggle she experienced living in a mixed marriage with her newly converted Roman Catholic husband. She wrote:

> I tried to fit into Scott's life as a Catholic. The week after Easter, Scott led a Bible study in our home and I sat in. When a young man was asked to open in prayer, he promptly led in a Hail Mary. I left the room in agony, fell on my knees in my bedroom and wept bitterly — how dare he say those words in my home, rubbing salt into my open wound from Scott's conversion! Later, I tried to rejoin them, but their comments and expressions of Catholic piety

---

[14] Ibid., pages 88, 89.

were overwhelming. Soon Scott moved the Bible study out of our home, for which I was most grateful. [15]

Eventually, Kimberly softened her position and agreed to attend Mass with her husband. She described the thoughts that went through her mind:

One evening, we had an opportunity to be at a Mass where there was a Eucharistic procession at the end. I had never seen this before. As I watched row after row of grown men and women kneel and bow when the monstrance passed by, I thought, these people believe that is the Lord, and not just bread and wine. If this is Jesus, that is the only appropriate response. If one should kneel before a king today, how much more before the King of Kings? The Lord of Lords? Is it safe not to kneel?

But I continued to ruminate, what if it's not? If that is not Jesus in the monstrance, then what they are doing is gross idolatry. So, is it safe to kneel? The situation highlighted what Scott had said all along: the Catholic Church is not just another denomination — it is either true or diabolical. [16]

As more time passed, Kimberly's Protestant perspective of the Eucharist and Mary gradually changed. Eventually she found herself, like her husband Scott, in the position where she had a Eucharistic encounter that changed her life. She writes:

During a prayer time the week before Easter, I was amazed how much the monstrance seemed to symbolize the Catholic Church. Like many Protes-

---

[15] Ibid., pages 105, 106.
[16] Ibid., page 142.

tants, I had been concerned about Mary, the saints, and the sacraments were roadblocks between believers and God so that to get to God, one would have to go around them. They seemed to complicate life with God unnecessarily — like accretions on the sides of sunken treasures, they had to be discarded to get to what was important.

But now I could see the opposite was true, Catholicism was not a distant religion, but a presence oriented one — Catholics were the ones who had Jesus physically present in churches and saw themselves as living tabernacles after receiving the Eucharist. And because Jesus is the Eucharist, keeping Him in the center allows all of the rich doctrines of the Church to emanate from him, just as the beautiful gold rays stream forth from the Host in the monstrance. [17]

Paul Thigpen

Paul Thigpen, Ph.D., is a senior editor for Servant Publications, associate editor of *Envoy Magazine*, and the best-selling author of more than twenty-five books. Thigpen is a former evangelical Protestant pastor who entered the Catholic Church in 1993. [18]

One of Thigpen's books is *Jesus We Adore You: Prayers before the Blessed Sacrament*. [19] In the introduction section of this book, Thigpen shares his testimony with regard to the importance of Eucharistic adoration and how it played a

---

[17] Ibid., page 162.
[18] Paul Thigpen, *The Rapture Trap: A Catholic Response to "End Times" Fever*, Ascension Press, West Chester, PA, 2001, back cover.
[19] Paul Thigpen, *Jesus We Adore You: Prayers Before the Blessed Sacrament*, Servant Publications, Ann Arbor, MI, 2001.

significant role in his personal conversion to Roman Catholicism:

> I felt it first as a longing, an ache that resisted all remedy, a hunger that refused to be filled. I was perplexed. What was in these Catholic churches that wooed me whenever I visited to pray.
>
> It was of course the Eucharistic Presence. But until I became Catholic myself and learned about that glorious, veiled Reality, I could only marvel at the peace, the joy, the strength I encountered whenever I knelt before the tabernacle. I was haunted by the hidden God.
>
> The day came at last when I actually tasted of the Bread of heaven—could any day have been happier?—and He joined Himself to me more intimately than I could ever have imagined. But in the years since, that Feast has only sharpened the hunger for Him; as many of the saints have observed, the more we feed on Him, the more we want.

More Eucharistic Encounters

More and more Protestants are testifying they are being drawn to the Catholic Church, especially through the Eucharist. Some say they have encountered the presence of Christ in a new and exciting way. One such person is Presbyterian pastor Steven Muse. Muse is one of the contributing authors of *Mary the Mother of All: Protestant Perspectives and Experiences of Medjugorje,* published by the Loyola University Press and edited by Sharon E. Cheston.

According to Muse, his visit to Medjugorje was life changing, especially after he encountered the Eucharistic Christ. He wrote:

> The fact remains that never before or since in my life have I had such an encounter with Christ in the

Eucharist. I believe this is because I never received the bread and the wine as the Body and the Blood of Christ, so what I loved in my heart and believed in my mind were never experienced as real in the here and now of my bodily presence as I encountered him again and again for the entire week. Sometimes this happened twice a day as I received Communion both in the morning at English Mass, and again in the evening at the Croatian Mass, where I did not even understand what they were saying or singing but only prayed the rosary in my own language with the others as if I had been saying "Hail Marys" all my life. What was true was that the Father, Son and Holy Spirit were real. And *Mary was real.* [20]

While Muse testified of a real encounter with "Christ" and then "Mary" while visiting Medjugorje, other well-known Protestants like Benny Hinn have made predictions that "Christ" will be showing up on stage at his crusades. On March 29, 2000 Hinn made the following statement on his television program:

The Holy Spirit has spoken, He told me He is about to show up. Oh, I gotta tell you this just before we go. I had a word of prophecy from Ruth Heflin, you know who Ruth Heflin is? Ruth prophesied over me back in the seventies. Everything she said has happened. She just sent me a word through my wife and said: The Lord spoke to her audibly and said, that He is going to appear physically in one of our crusades in the next few months. Yeah, She... I'm telling ya she said, the Lord spoke to her audi-

---

[20] Sharon E. Cheston, *Mary The Mother of All: Protestant Perspectives and Experiences of Medjugorje,* Loyola University Press, Chicago, 1992, page 57. [emphasis in the original]

bly and said, tell Benny I'm going to appear physically on the platform in his meetings. Lord, do it in
Phoenix, Arizona in the name of Jesus! And in
Kenya too, Lord, please, Lord, in fact, do it in every
crusade in Jesus' name. [21]

For those who have followed the ministry of Benny
Hinn, the previous statement should come as no great
surprise. Hinn had previously claimed that "Jesus" mate-
rialized to him during a Catholic Mass while he was par-
ticipating in Communion at a Catholic Church in
Amarillo, Texas. Speaking with Paul Crouch on a Trinity
Broadcasting Network "Praise the Lord Program" on December 24, 1997 Hinn described this experience:

> The next thing I was feeling was actually the form
> of a body, the shape of a body. And my
> body...went totally numb. ...And God really gave
> me a revelation that night, that when we partake
> communion, it's not just communion, Paul
> [Crouch]. We are partaking Christ Jesus himself.
> He did not say, "Take, eat, this *represents* my
> body." He said, "This *is* my body, broken for
> you..." When you partake communion, you're
> partaking Christ, and that heals your body. When
> you partake Jesus how can you stay weak?...sick?
> ...And so tonight, as we partake communion, we're
> not partaking bread. We're partaking what *He* said
> we would be partaking of: "This is my *body*." [22]

While Benny Hinn would not be considered a Roman
Catholic by his followers, the previous statement indicates

---

[21] Benny Hinn with Steve Brock "This is Your Day" television
broadcast, 700 Club Studios, Virginia Beach, VA, March 29, 2000.

[22] *Praise The Lord Show*, Trinity Broadcasting Network, December
27, 1994. [emphasis added.]

he has been influenced by the Roman Catholic teaching of the Eucharistic Christ. Hinn's ministry has had a powerful influence on people all over the world. It will be interesting to see if his acceptance of transubstantiation and the Presence of Christ in the Eucharist will become more and more apparent.

Healing Roman Catholic Style

While several testimonies documented in the first part of this chapter have already revealed how various individuals have been drawn to the Roman Catholic Church, the following testimony explains how a Pentecostal pastor was converted to Roman Catholicism and how he now uses the Eucharist in his "healing" ministry.

On March 4, 2004, Michael Brown posted an article on his Spirit Daily web site titled "Former Pentecostal Relates Miracle that Occurred With the Precious Blood."

This article is about former pastor, Dr. Bob Rice, a Pentecostal pastor of thirty-three years who was converted to Catholicism. Brown begins his article the following way:

> When his first wife died and he remarried, it was to a Catholic woman, and this eventually led to his conversion—and a continuation of the remarkable events. Those at his Pentecostal church wouldn't accept his wife, and so he left and began exclusively attending Catholic Mass. About three months after resigning from his church, he began feeling uncomfortable that he couldn't receive Communion, and so he began his journey into Catholicism. [23]

---

[23] Michael Brown, "Former Pentecostal Relates Miracle that Occurred With the Precious Blood," http://www.spiritdaily.com/rice2.htm, cited March 3, 2004.

At first Dr. Rice was not convinced that Christ's actual "Real Presence" occurred when the priest consecrated the bread and wine. He considered it to be symbolic. However, his views began to change. Brown, writing about Dr. Rice's experience stated:

> "The Lord began dealing with me that this occurs when the Catholic priest consecrates," he says. When he asked why a Protestant minister couldn't do the same, he says, it was given to him that only a priest can do so because a priest is in the apostolic line of succession. "It's because a priest is in that succession that he has the authority to pray over the bread and wine," says Dr. Rice. [24]

After Dr. Rice had been a Catholic for about a year, he had a supernatural encounter with the "exposition of the Blessed Sacrament." Brown writes:

It was after being a Catholic for about a year that Rice, a former truck driver and pastor of six churches, happened to encounter exposition of the Blessed Sacrament. "Now what is *this*?" thought the former minister, who still possessed a few anti-Catholic biases — and still had his doubts about the real Presence. But they were to be dispelled that day. "As I sat there looking at the Blessed Sacrament, all of a sudden the face of Christ appeared to me in the center of the Blessed Sacrament," he asserts. "I said, 'All right, Lord, I get the picture!'" [25]

According to Michael Brown, Dr. Rice has been transformed from a Pentecostal Protestant with a healing ministry, to a Roman Catholic who performs healings before the Blessed Sacrament. But that is not all. According to Brown:

---

[24] Ibid.
[25] Ibid.

Rice sees the Catholic Church as a "sleeping giant." "The longer I'm Catholic and the more I study it, the more I become absolutely convinced that the Catholic Church is awesome," says the former Protestant. "The Catholic Church always has been *the* apostolic church—and we ought to be acting like it. Signs and wonders and miracles and everything that took place in the Church 2,000 years ago should be happening today, because the Church hasn't changed. [26]

Since becoming a Roman Catholic healer, Rice has changed his healing strategy. Rice states:

I do everything I can now to lead people to the Eucharist for healing. My main message is being healed through the Mass, because if Jesus is truly present in the Eucharist—which He is—and if Jesus is God—which He is—and if God can't be separated from His power, which He can't, then that same power that was available 2,000 years ago, that caused the blind to see and the deaf to hear and the lame to walk, that power that cast out devils, cleansed the lepers, and raised the dead, that power that spoke this entire universe into existence, is also present in the Holy Eucharist because Jesus *is* the Holy Eucharist. [27]

Finally, Michael Brown described an experience that Dr. Rice had while attending Mass at a church in Florida. Perhaps this experience provides a glimpse of where experience-based Christianity may be headed in the future:

At the cathedral in Venice, Florida, Dr. Rice says that the pastor dropped a Host without knowing it,

---

[26] Ibid.
[27] Ibid.

as he was administering Communion to one of the servers. It fell out of the ciborium without his noticing it. "So when Anita and I went up to receive Communion, I leaned over to the priest and said, 'Father, you dropped Jesus on the floor.' He got this blank look on his face, just stunned, and I said, 'May I have the privilege of rescuing Our Lord from the floor?' and he said, 'Yes, of course.'

"And so I went up to the sanctuary area, leaned over, and picked Jesus up off the floor, then went back down around the front of the altar and bowed before the altar and consumed the Eucharist. I went back to my seat and sat down and then knelt forward.

"When I did, a flood of the Presence of God hit me like I have never felt in my life. Never have I felt His Presence like that time. I was bouncing off the walls for three hours. It was just awesome." And this former Pentecostal knows why: "When we consume the Holy Eucharist," he says, "we are consuming the God Who spoke this entire universe into existence." [28]

Rescuing Idols?

It appears that Dr. Rice and many others are basing their beliefs on a powerful experience rather than on the Bible and just plain common sense. In the Bible we find that idols can be stolen, fall down and even need to be rescued. In the Book of Genesis, when Laban learned that his idols had been stolen he accused Jacob saying: "Why did you steal my gods?" [29]

---

[28] Ibid.
[29] Genesis 31:30

And when the Philistines brought the Ark of the Covenant into the temple of their god Dagon, their idol of Dagon repeatedly fell down to the ground. The Philistines attempted to rescue the idol of Dagon from the ground and set it back in its place, only to find it fallen and broken again the next morning. [30]

Isaiah, chapters 40 through 46, represent perhaps the most thorough biblical contrast between the Almighty God who created all and upholds all, versus the vain idols of the heathen. I would recommend that you read these chapters and ask yourself whether the Eucharistic Christ is the true and living God, or more like the useless idols worshipped and fashioned with men's hands. Of course the true God does not need to be rescued. On the contrary, we need to be rescued by Him.

Experience-based Christianity

In this chapter we have examined several testimonies from individuals who have had an encounter with the Eucharistic Christ. We have seen how the New Evangelization program presently underway is definitely showing signs of success. Numerous other testimonies could be presented that confirm a mystical addictive spiritual power that seems to be drawing people to the Eucharistic Christ.

As we have seen, in almost every conversion account there is a common denominator. Each person who has converted to the Catholic Church has done so based on profound, powerful, and often gratifying experiences. These people were drawn by a feeling that they were missing some deeper spiritual encounter. They all acknowledge some sort of sensation that was genuinely fulfilling.

---

[30] 1 Samuel 5:1-5

It is obvious that a definite trend is underway. An experienced-based Christianity that is focused on signs and wonders associated with spiritual encounters pointing to the Eucharistic Christ and/or his mother, the Mother of the Eucharist.

But there is another powerful influence that has not yet been investigated. There are numerous accounts from around the world that a woman has been appearing in the form of an apparition who is drawing attention to her son, the Eucharistic Christ. This woman, who Catholics call the Queen of Heaven, is supposedly the mother of Jesus.

Whether or not there will be massive conversions to the Roman Catholic Church in the future, time will tell. One thing is for certain, there are plenty of individuals claiming they have received messages and inspiration from the spirit world that predict the reign of the Eucharistic Christ and his mother is just around the corner.

Chapter Ten
The "Mary" Connection

As you read through the Old and New Testament, one thing becomes very apparent. Christianity is all about Jesus Christ. "For God so loved the world that He gave His only begotten Son, that whoever believes in Him should not perish but have everlasting life. [1] Christianity is all about believing in Jesus alone. It is the Scriptures that testify of the true Jesus. Jesus made this clear:

> You search the Scriptures, for in them you think you have eternal life; and these are they which testify of Me. But you are not willing to come to Me that you may have life. [2]

The entire Bible leads us to, testifies of, and focuses on, the one and only Savior of the world.

> Philip found Nathanael and said to him, "We have found Him of whom Moses in the law, and also the prophets, wrote—Jesus of Nazareth, the son of Joseph." [3]

---

[1] John 3:16
[2] John 5:39-40
[3] John 1:45

And beginning at Moses and all the Prophets, [Jesus] expounded to them in all the Scriptures the things concerning Himself. [4]

Adding to God's Word or perverting His Word has devastating results. To do so, or follow those who do, is very dangerous. In the very last chapter of the Bible we read this somber warning:

For I testify to everyone who hears the words of the prophecy of this book: If anyone adds to these things, God will add to him the plagues that are written in this book; and if anyone takes away from the words of the book of this prophecy, God shall take away his part from the Book of Life... [5]

According to the Bible, if you follow a false christ based on unscriptural sources you will end up separated from the true Christ, and spend eternity in hell.

The Catholic "Mary" Points to the Eucharistic Christ

Earlier in this book, quotes were made from an article published by *Zenit* on April 17, 2003. This article reported that Pope John Paul II had called for Catholics to refocus on the Eucharist and Eucharistic adoration from an encyclical that he had written called "Ecclesia de Eucharistia." On the very same day, *Zenit* sent out another news item that was equally important. The title for this article was "Mary Has a Place in Latest Encyclical: Pope Describes Her as a 'Woman of the Eucharist.'" [6]

The article began the following way: "The last chapter of John Paul's encyclical "Ecclesia de Eucharistia" is dedicated to the Virgin Mary—a surprise in a document dedi-

---

[4] Luke 24:27
[5] Revelation 22:18-19
[6] http://www.zenit.org/english/visualizza.phtml?sid=34405.

cated to the Blessed Sacrament." [7] Then this interesting statement from the pope's 14th encyclical: "If the Church and the Eucharist are inseparably united, the same ought to be said of Mary and the Eucharist." [8]

Then laying a foundation for the Catholic Church that is not found anywhere in Scripture, *Zenit* quoted the pope:

> The relationship between the Virgin Mary and the Eucharist is explained by referring to the "Eucharistic faith" that Mary already practiced "even before the institution of the Eucharist, by the very fact that she offered her virginal womb for the incarnation of God's Word." [9]

The article then concluded with another profound statement made by the pope:

> "Mary is present with the Church and as Mother of the Church, at each of our celebrations of the Eucharist. Mary Most Holy, in whom the Eucharistic mystery shows itself more than in anyone else, as mystery of light." [10]

Think about the implications of this statement! According to the head of the Roman Catholic Church, when the ordained priest consecrates the wafer during Mass, not only does "Jesus" appear, but the mother of "Jesus" also shows up. Of course, those who have read the Bible know that only God is omnipresent.

It can be documented that a woman claiming to be the mother of Jesus has been appearing in numerous places all over the world for some time. While I touched on this

---

[7] Ibid.
[8] Ibid.
[9] Ibid.
[10] Ibid.

subject in a previous book *New Wine and the Babylonian Vine*, a more thorough and complete exposition of this topic can be found in *Messages from Heaven* authored by Jim Tetlow. This book reveals that the "Mary" of the apparitions, and the Catholic Church, is not the Mary of the Bible. (Refer to the back of this book for more information.)

Those who follow the apparitions are very aware there is a "Mary-Eucharist" connection that is extremely important. The rest of this chapter will document this connection based on information that has been made available from appendix A found in the back of the book, *Messages from Heaven* by Jim Tetlow.

Peace through Eucharistic Devotion

Throughout the world, the apparition of Mary is emphasizing the importance of the Eucharist. With the increasing number of Marian apparitions, there has been a corresponding increase in Eucharistic adoration. [11] This is no surprise to the millions who are devoted to the "Blessed Mother." Those who follow her messages are aware of an interesting prediction made by Catholic Saint John Bosco in 1862.

> There will be chaos in the Church. Tranquility will not return until the Pope succeeds in anchoring the boat of Peter between the twin pillars of Eucharistic devotion and devotion to Our Lady. This will come about one year before the end of the [20th] century.[12]

---

[11] Eucharistic Adoration is the worship and prayer offered by Roman Catholics and others to Jesus in the Eucharist, when kneeling in front of the displayed consecrated Communion Host.

[12] Saint John Bosco, 1862. Refer to: members.aol.com/bjw1106/Euchmir.htm.

Many believe that this prophecy is near fulfillment. For instance, in more recent years, the apparition has encouraged the formation of Perpetual Eucharistic Adoration groups. These groups number in the thousands around the world. [13] Their sole purpose is to worship, adore, and pray to Jesus in the Eucharist around the clock, perpetually.

Eucharistic and Marian Era

Of course, Marian apparitions have always stressed the great importance of the Eucharist. In particular, the Queen of Heaven has repeatedly stated that the Eucharist, once consecrated by a priest, becomes the literal body, blood, soul, and divinity of Jesus, and is therefore worthy of worship and adoration. For example, "Mary" focused much attention on her Son's true presence in the Eucharist in the now famous apparitions to Catherine Laboure at Rue du Bac, Paris in 1830.

Marian theologians consistently agree that the revelations in Paris in 1830 to Catherine Laboure, officially began an era of Mary. That this apparition had a Eucharistic theme is consistent with the increasing number of apparitions that have appeared in the nineteenth, twentieth and now, twenty-first centuries. In fact, nearly every popular apparition today stresses the importance of the Eucharist. "Mary" emphatically encourages all believers to receive the Blessed Sacrament as often as possible in order to receive the needed graces for salvation. She also stresses the important role that the Eucharistic Jesus will have in the last days.

---

[13] "The Real Presence Association: Churches and Chapels that have Eucharistic Adoration," Online posting, http://www.therealpresence.org/chap_fr.htm, cited April 20, 2002. This web site lists over 6,500 adoration sites in the US alone.

In conjunction with these messages, many "Eucharistic miracles" have been reported. These miracles include bleeding and pulsating Communion Hosts, Hosts that do not decompose, Hosts that speak, and Hosts that transform into the image of a man—presumably Jesus. Tests at several apparition sites confirm that the blood emanating from miraculous Hosts is authentic. These miracles are presented as proof by the apparition that Christ is truly present under the appearance of the consecrated Communion wafer.

Our Lady of Fatima Emphasizes the Eucharist

Those who espouse the Marian apparitions are united in their belief that the apparitions have, over the centuries, increasingly pointed to the central importance of the Eucharist. For instance, Dr. Thomas W. Petrisko dedicates his book *Mother of the Secret* to exploring this interesting link between key Marian apparitions and Eucharistic prominence. Below is his summary of the Fatima apparitions:

> The Apparitions of the Blessed Virgin Mary in Fatima, Portugal in 1917 to three shepherd children are most remembered for the incredible signs and secrets given there. Yet it must be said that Heaven truly marked the events with a significant thrust to focus the attention of the faithful on the True Presence of Jesus Christ in the Eucharist. ...In 1916, one year before the Virgin Mary's first apparition, ...the children received an apparition of an angel holding a chalice in his left hand. A Host was suspended above the chalice and some drops of blood from the Host fell into the chalice. Leaving the chalice suspended in the air, the angel knelt down beside the children and told them to repeat three times the following prayer: "O Most Holy Trinity, Father,

Son, and Holy Spirit...I offer Thee the most precious Body, Blood, Soul, and Divinity of Jesus
Christ, present in all the tabernacles of the world,
in reparation for [sins]..." [14]

The Eucharist Holds Center Stage in Medjugorje

There is undeniably a strong devotion to the Eucharist
at the Fatima apparition site. However, the Queen of
Heaven's Eucharistic emphasis at Medjugorje is arguably
greater. Our Lady of Medjugorje has time after time told
visionaries to worship and adore Jesus in the Eucharist
and to frequently partake in Holy Communion. Medjugorje visionary Vicka Ivankovic tells us what the
"Blessed Mother" explained to her about Christ's true
presence in the Eucharist:

The Blessed Mother says that during each Mass, Jesus comes in person, in tangible form. We can take
Jesus, in physical form, into our body...This is our
way to accept Jesus into our heart. Jesus comes
alive to us through the Eucharist. [15]

Those who have visited Medjugorje or examined Our
Lady's messages are convinced that the apparition teaches
that the Eucharist is the source and summit of Catholic life.
For instance, the late Father Joseph A. Pelletier, A.A., a
noted theologian, wrote in his book, *The Queen of Peace
Visits Medjugorje*, that the central theme of the Medjugorje
apparitions is primarily Eucharistic:

As more and more information has come forth, it
has become increasingly clear that the Eucharist
holds center stage in Medjugorje and that from the

---

[14] Thomas W. Petrisko, *Mother of the Secret*, Santa Barbara, CA,
Queenship Publishing, 1997, page 113.
[15] Ibid., pages 185, 186.

very start Our Lady spoke to the six seers about the Eucharist and its importance with more frequency than was suspected. This helps to understand why the parish has placed so much emphasis on the Mass and public adoration of the Blessed Sacrament. [16]

Our Lady of Medjugorje Leads to the Eucharist

Father Rene Laurentin in his book, *Is the Virgin Mary Appearing at Medjugorje?*, concurs with Fr. Pelletier about Medjugorje and the Eucharist. Fr. Laurentin writes:

Our Lady of Medjugorje leads to Christ. When she was asked which prayer is the best, she answered: "It is the Mass, and you will never be able to exhaust its greatness. That is why you should be there humbly and prepared." At Medjugorje the Virgin leads to the Eucharist. The Rosary and the apparition flow into the Mass. Mary has sometimes appeared showing Christ, in His childhood (the first apparition and Christmas 1983) or in His Passion. In showing us Christ, she continues to say, "Do whatever he tells you." (John 2:5) [17]

Of course the most important part of the Mass is the sacrifice of the Mass, where Christ is offered in the Eucharist. Not only does Our Lady of Medjugorje encourage the faithful to attend Mass and partake in the Blessed Sacrament frequently, but she also promotes the adoration and worship of the consecrated Communion Host.

Dear children, I am especially grateful that you are here tonight. Adore unceasingly the Most Blessed

---

[16] Fr. Joseph A. Pelletier, *The Queen of Peace Visits Medjugorje,* Worchester, MA, Assumption Publications, 1985, page 205.
[17] Petrisko, page 187.

Sacrament of the altar. Know that I am always present when the faithful are adoring. [18]

Dear children, today I invite you to fall in love with the most Holy Sacrament of the Altar. Adore Him, little children, in your parishes, and in this way you will be united with the entire world. [19]

Garabandal Emphasizes the Eucharist

Messages given by the apparition of Mary who appeared in Garabandal, Spain echo those given at Medjugorje.

We must pay visit to the Blessed Sacrament. Many sacrifices must be made. Much penance must be done. But first of all we must be good...If we do not do this, punishment awaits us.... [20]

In his book, *Mother of the Secret*, Dr. Thomas W. Petrisko writes the following regarding the importance of the Eucharist at Garabandal, Spain:

While the alleged supernatural character and prophetic element of the apparitions at Garabandal are noted, its message is interpreted by many experts as being predominantly Eucharistic. This opinion is enhanced by the fact that the visionaries were

---

[18] Richard J. Beyer, *Medjugorje Day By Day*, Notre Dame, IN, Ave Maria Press, July 18th meditation, Message from Our Lady of Medjugorje given on March 15, 1984.

[19] "Our Lady of Medjugorje," Online posting, http://medjugorje.org/msg95.htm, cited Sept. 28, 1998, Message from Our Lady of Medjugorje, Sept. 25, 1995.

[20] "Garabandal - Pines Will Enlighten The World," Online posting, http://here.at/garabandal/pines.htm, cited May 15, 2000, Message from Our Lady of Garabandal given on October 18, 1961. Error in original quote.

photographed receiving upon their tongues invisible and then visible communion Hosts from an an-
gel. [21]

Ted and Maureen Flynn, in their book, *The Thunder of
Justice,* agree that Garabandal has a predominately Eucharistic theme:

> Another remarkable event of Garabandal empha-
> sized the importance of the Eucharist. An angel
> appeared bearing a golden chalice. The angel asked
> the children to think of the One whom they were
> going to receive. He taught them to recite the Con-
> fiteor, after which he gave them Holy Communion.
> He also taught them to say the Anima Christi in
> thanksgiving. These direct interventions occurred
> regularly whenever the priest from the neighboring
> village of Cosio was unable to come to Garaban-
> dal. [22]

Everywhere "Mary" Emphasizes the Eucharist

Apparitions from the four corners of the globe express
this common and central theme. The Eucharist has the
power to transform the world. The Eucharist should be
worshipped. Eucharistic adoration will bring peace and
unity. Messages originating from such diverse places as
Amsterdam, Holland; Akita, Japan; Rome, Italy; Naju, Korea; Bayside, New York, and Budapest, Hungary all con-
vey this common idea. What follows are a sampling of the
numerous messages from apparitions emphasizing the
great importance of the Eucharist.

---

[21] Petrisko, page 157.
[22] Ted and Maureen Flynn, *Thunder of Justice,* Sterling, VA,
MaxKol Communications, Inc., 1993, page 164.

Our Lady has been appearing in private to Marisa Rossi in Rome. In June 1993 She asked...that Her messages about the Eucharist be made public....Our Lady says: "I am THE MOTHER OF THE EUCHARIST" and She wants to spread renewed and strong devotion, all over the world, for this great Sacrament. [23]

During Consecration I suddenly saw a light coming from the chalice...

When I went to Holy Communion and returned to my place, the Sacred Host began to move on my tongue and I heard the voice of the Lady say, "You have now met the Lord." [24]

You must firmly believe that Jesus is truly present in the Host as Man and God! You must believe that you really meet Him, and, more than that, unite with Him in the Eucharist. [25]

My Son will always be there in the Eucharist. A duly ordained and consecrated hand of a legal representative, your priest, will always be able to bring to you My Son's Body and Blood in the

---

[23] "Our Lady is Appearing in Rome," "Messages of the Mother of the Eucharist," Online posting, http://www.geocities.com/Athens/Forum/6832/, cited February 16, 2000. Messages to the visionary Marisa Rossi.

[24] Josef Kunzli, editor, *The Messages of The Lady of All Nations,* Santa Barbara, CA, Queenship Publishing, 1996, page 110. Message given on May 31, 1967.

[25] Peter Heintz, *A Guide to Apparitions*, Sacramento, CA, Gabriel Press, 1995, page 219. Message from Our Lady to visionary Sister Dolores of Budapest, Hungary.

Eucharist....He comes to you physically and spiritually.... [26]

Do you say well the prayer of the Handmaids of the Eucharist? Then let us pray it together. "Most Sacred Heart of Jesus, truly present in Holy Eucharist, I consecrate my body and soul to be entirely one with Your Heart, being sacrificed at every instant on all the altars of the world and giving praise to the Father pleading for the coming of His Kingdom." [27]

In these days you will hear of many Eucharistic Phenomena taking place. You will be renewed in your total reverence for my Divine Son in the Blessed Sacrament, and soon the time will come when the Tabernacle is returned to its rightful and proper place in the church. [28]

I have manifested the images of the Holy Eucharist in various ways so that all my children may understand the importance of the Holy Eucharist. Hurriedly become blazing flames of love, reparation

---

[26] "Our Lady of the Roses - Bayside Prophecies," Volume 1, page 299, Online posting,
http://www.roses.org/prophecy/seqevnt.htm, cited October 1, 1998, messages from Our Lady of the Roses to Veronica Lueken, Dec. 23, 1974, Bayside, NY.
[27] Teiji Yasuda, O.S.V., English version by John M. Haffert, *Akita: The Tears and Message of Mary*, Asbury, NJ, 101 Foundation, Inc., 1989, pages 194, 195. Message from Our Lady of Akita, Japan to Sr. Agnes Sasagawa, July 6, 1973.
[28] "Apparitions of Jesus and Mary," Online posting,
http://web.frontier.net/Apparitions/Cain.msgs94.html, cited February 16, 2000. Messages from Our Lady to Cyndi Cain, USA, Sept. 8, 1994.

and adoration toward the Lord Who is in the Blessed Sacrament. [29]

The Eucharistic Reign of Jesus

Furthermore, the apparition of Mary explains that the culmination of her apparitions will usher in the Eucharistic Reign of Jesus. To Father Gobbi, the head of the Marian Movement of Priests, she proclaims that the Eucharistic Jesus will soon transform humanity!

Today I ask all to throw open the doors to Jesus Christ who is coming. I am the Mother of the Second Advent and the door which is being opened on the new era. This new era will coincide with the greatest triumph of the Eucharistic Reign of Jesus. For this, I invite you, in this extraordinary year, to make flourish everywhere the cult of adoration, of reparation and of love for the Most Holy Eucharist....Let the Eucharist become the center of your prayer, of your life.... [30]

In fact, the coming of the glorious reign of Christ will coincide with the greatest splendor of his Eucharistic reign among you. The Eucharistic Jesus will release all his power of love, which will transform souls, the Church and all humanity. [31]

---

[29] "The Story of Naju," Online posting, http://www.nd.edu/~mary/Naju.html, cited May 15, 2000. Messages from the Blessed Mother to Julia Kim, Naju, Korea, June 27, 1993.
[30] Fr. Don Stefano Gobbi, *To the Priests, Our Lady's Beloved Sons*, St. Francis ME, The National Headquarters of the Marian Movement of Priests in the United States of America, 1998, page 676. Message given to Father Gobbi, February 26, 1991, Brazil.
[31] Ibid., page 640. Message given to Father Gobbi, April 12, 1990, Italy.

The glorious reign of Christ will coincide with the triumph of the Eucharistic reign of Christ....Jesus will be made manifest above all in the mystery of his Eucharistic presence. [32]

Establishing the Link

Marian experts agree that the triumph of "Mary's" immaculate heart, prophesied at Fatima, will be directly linked to perpetual adoration of the Blessed Sacrament. Father Martin Lucia, writing in the journal, *Immaculata*, explains that all the Marian apparitions will victoriously culminate in the Eucharistic reign of Jesus.

> The message of all the Marian apparitions, both past and present, is that the triumph of the Immaculate Heart of Mary will culminate in the Eucharistic reign of the Sacred Heart of Jesus. The Eucharistic Reign will come through perpetual adoration of Jesus in the Blessed Sacrament. [33]

Not surprisingly, the pope himself alludes to this consummation of apparitions in his encyclical, *Mother of the Redeemer*:

> The piety of the Christian people has always very rightly sensed a profound link between devotion to the Blessed Virgin and worship of the Eucharist: This is a fact that can be seen in the liturgy of both the West and the East, in the traditions of the religious families, in the modern movements of spirituality, including those for youth, and in the

---

[32] Paul A. Mihalik, *The Virgin Mary, Fr. Gobbi and the Year 2000,* Santa Barbara, CA, 1998, page 29. Message to Father Gobbi, given on November 21, 1993, Australia. [bold not in original]
[33] Thomas W. Petrisko, *Mother of the Secret,* page 268.

pastoral practice of the Marian shrines. Mary guides the faithful to the Eucharist. [34]

Eucharistic Miracles

Of course, the humble Mary of the Bible never once referred to the Eucharist. Nor did she ever instruct Christ's followers to worship the Eucharist. However, this survey of messages given by the "Mother of the Eucharist" around the world, shows that the apparition that claims to be Mary consistently directs followers to concentrate on Christ's Real Presence in the Eucharist. And as if to corroborate "Mary's" messages, at many of these apparition sites, Eucharistic miracles, such as bleeding Communion Hosts have occurred.

For example, in Betania, Venezuela, the location of a popular Marian apparition, a bleeding Communion Host was analyzed chemically. The analyzed sample was found to be human blood. Here is a summary of the Betania Eucharistic miracle as recorded in the book, *Cenacle Formation Manual and Prayer Book*. This book is distributed by the Eucharistic Apostles of Divine Mercy, and chronicles many Eucharistic miracles:

> All the miracles listed occurred several hundred years ago. But the miracle that occurred during Mass in Betania, Venezuela took place on the feast of the Immaculate Conception in 1991. A Consecrated Host, truly the flesh of Our Lord, began to bleed. A subsequent medical team concluded that the material extruded from the Host was blood of human origin. The local bishop declared it a sign of transubstantiation saying, "God is trying to mani-

---

[34] Pope John Paul II, "Redemptoris Mater, Mother of the Redeemer," *Origins Volume 16*, Washington, DC, March 25, 1987, page 762, encyclical. [bold not in original]

fest to us that our faith in the consecrated Host is authentic."

Many other extraordinary events have occurred in Betania, including numerous alleged apparitions of the Blessed Mother witnessed by several thousand people, multiple physical and spiritual healings, and a mystic named Maria Esperanza who has the gifts of stigmata, bilocation, and levitation during prayer. The bishop himself has witnessed the phenomena and wrote in a pastoral letter that after careful study, he has declared the apparitions authentic and of supernatural character. [35]

Many more examples could be cited. For example, in Stich, Germany a bleeding Host that stained the altar cloth was chemically analyzed at the Polyclinical Institute of the University of Zurich. No one at the institute was made aware of the source of the stains. The stains were analyzed by four different methods of chemical identification and in each case the findings were the same—the stains were human blood. [36]

Apparitions of "Jesus" Confirm the Eucharistic Christ

If "Mary's" apparitions don't convince the skeptic, and if miracles aren't enough to persuade the cynic, then there is an even stronger validation offered by the faithful. Apparitions of "Jesus" himself are appearing. Yes, apparitions of "Jesus" have also been reported worldwide, albeit

---

[35] Bryan and Susan Thatcher; Seraphim Michalenko, M.I.C., *Cenacle Formation Manual and Prayer Book*, Stockbridge, MA, The Association of Marian Helpers, 1999, page 81.

[36] "Betania - I come to reconcile them," Online posting, http://members.aol.com/bjw1106/marian9.htm, cited August 28, 1998.

at a much lower frequency, and they too give attention to the true presence of Jesus in the Eucharist.

> At St. Andrew's Church, Edmonton, Alberta, Canada, after Communion, I could see the Host in the monstrance and then it was quickly covered over. Jesus said: "My dear people, today you celebrate My institution of My Blessed Sacrament by My Presence coming into the bread and wine at the Mass. Believe, My faithful, that I am truly present in the consecrated bread and wine. You have witnessed many miracles of My Real Blood coming forth from the Host as evidence to those unbelievers. I tell you, at every Mass you witness My miracle in the Transubstantiation when the bread and wine are made into My Body and Blood. Take advantage of this time to adore Me in exposition of My Host, for a time is coming when this privilege will be taken away. I recommend to all of you to encourage your priests to have Perpetual Adoration of My Host. I bring many graces to those who can visit Me and give Me praise and adoration." [37]

> Many of the miracles have been proven to be Real Blood by the scientists. Even in the face of reality and technical proof, there are still many who do not believe in My Real Presence. This denial of My Presence is the worst of insults and a disrespect for My Gift of the Eucharist. This is why those same people, who reject My Presence, do not feel it necessary to confess their sins. Those, who teach against My Real Presence, and put down these miracles, are the real blasphemers....Those, who do

---

[37] John Leary, *Prepare for the Great Tribulation and the Era of Peace, Volume VII,* Santa Barbara, CA, Queenship Publishing, 1997, pages 57, 58. Message from "Jesus" to John Leary.

not love My Blessed Sacrament, are the lukewarm that I will vomit from My mouth. [38]

Why the Eucharist?

There are many more Eucharistic messages and reported miracles. But the question we must ask is why? Why does the apparition of Mary encourage the faithful to worship and adore the consecrated Host? Her many messages on the Eucharist have spurred the formation of multiplied thousands of Eucharistic prayer groups and perpetual Eucharistic adoration groups throughout the world. Was this her goal? Obviously yes! But might she have a much greater goal in mind?

In the book *Messages From Heaven*, author Jim Tetlow demonstrates from God's inerrant Word that the apparition of Mary contradicts the Scriptures and offers a false gospel. She, or more accurately it, is not the Mary of the Bible, but rather a satanic counterfeit. Therefore, would a demon endeavor to lead the world to worship and trust the true Jesus of the Bible? Or is it more likely that these impostors would direct the people of the world to worship "another Jesus" or a false christ?

In this chapter we have added another large piece to the overall puzzle. It is apparent that attention to the Eucharistic Christ is being focused not only by the pope, but also from apparitions claiming to be the mother of Jesus. Could their vision of a global move toward the Eucharistic Jesus really occur?

---

[38] Ibid., Volume XI, page 8. [bold not in original]

Chapter Eleven
The Eucharistic Reign of Christ

Jesus Christ can be found throughout the Bible, from Genesis to Revelation. The Old Testament prophesied of the coming Messiah hundreds of years before Jesus was born. The Bible predicted that the Savior would be born in Bethlehem. [1] He would be born of a virgin. [2] He would be fully God and fully Man. [3] He would be of the seed of Abraham. [4] He would be a descendant of King David. [5] He would live a sinless life. [6] He would be crucified and die for our sins. [7] He would rise from the dead. [8] He would ascend to heaven. [9]

The New Testament and history confirms that Jesus fulfilled all these prophecies and many more. We are also

---

[1] Micah 5:2
[2] Isaiah 7:14
[3] Isaiah 9:6-7
[4] Genesis 12:3; 22:18
[5] Jeremiah 23:5-6
[6] Isaiah 53:9, 11
[7] Psalm 22:16; Zechariah 12:10; Isaiah 52:13-53:12
[8] Psalm 16:10; 49:15; Malachi 4:2
[9] Psalm 68:18

told that after Jesus rose from the dead He appeared bodily to His disciples and many others before ascending bodily to heaven:

> For I delivered to you first of all that which I also received: that Christ died for our sins according to the Scriptures, and that He was buried, and that He rose again the third day according to the Scriptures, and that He was seen by Cephas, then by the twelve. After that He was seen by over five hundred brethren at once, of whom the greater part remain to the present, but some have fallen asleep.[10]

> And He led them out as far as Bethany, and He lifted up His hands and blessed them. Now it came to pass, while He blessed them, that He was parted from them and carried up into heaven. [11]

> Now when He had spoken these things, while they watched, He was taken up, and a cloud received Him out of their sight. [12]

The Word of God states that Jesus is currently at the right hand of the Father and that He is coming again:

> But this Man, after He had offered one sacrifice for sins forever, sat down at the right hand of God, from that time waiting till His enemies are made His footstool. [13]

> God, who at various times and in various ways spoke in time past to the fathers by the prophets, has in these last days spoken to us by His Son,

---

[10] 1 Corinthians 15:3-6
[11] Luke 24:50-51
[12] Acts 1:9
[13] Hebrews 10:12-13

whom He has appointed heir of all things, through whom also He made the worlds; who being the brightness of His glory and the express image of His person, and upholding all things by the word of His power, **when He had by Himself purged our sins, sat down at the right hand of the Majesty on high.** [14]

And while they looked steadfastly toward heaven as He went up, behold, two men stood by them in white apparel, who also said, "Men of Galilee, why do you stand gazing up into heaven? This same Jesus, who was taken up from you into heaven, will so come in like manner as you saw Him go into heaven." [15]

Second Coming or Manifestation?

The previous statements about Jesus are all supported by Scripture. However, despite the overwhelming evidence, not everyone who claims to be a Christian agrees with the literal interpretation of these Bible verses. In particular, there are those who believe Jesus will manifest in His Eucharistic presence before He rules and reigns in His glorified body.

In this chapter, we want to examine what role the Eucharistic Christ may play with regard to the Second Coming of "Jesus" and the last days. The Bible clearly teaches that the Second Coming of Christ will be in a moment of time and that every person on earth will simultaneously witness Jesus return:

Behold, He is coming with clouds, and every eye will see Him, even they who pierced Him. And all

---

[14] Hebrews 1:1-3
[15] Acts 1:10-11

the tribes of the earth will mourn because of Him. Even so, Amen. [16]

However, teachings associated with the Eucharistic Christ appear to be preparing the world for an alternative Second Coming scenario often called the Eucharistic Reign of Jesus.

Apparitions of "Jesus"

Michael Brown is an investigative journalist. His conversion experience took place in 1983. Since that date he has visited twenty-five sites of alleged Marian apparitions around the world. He has authored numerous books and his articles have appeared in periodicals such as *Reader's Digest, New York Magazine, The Atlantic Monthly, Discover,* and *The New York Times.* [17]

Brown's web site is Spirit Daily. Each day he posts articles that relate to current events and his view of Bible prophecy. Many of his commentaries deal with topics related to Marian apparitions and the role he believes these apparitions play in preparing the world for what lies ahead. Brown also writes extensively on the topic of the Eucharist and conveys the message that we are about to enter into a new era characterized by what is known as the Eucharistic Reign of Christ.

On July 1, 2003, Spirit Daily posted two articles dealing with the subject of Christ and the future. One article was titled "Manifestation of Jesus Could Take Form That's Similar to Full-Scale Apparitions." This is how the article began:

---

[16] Revelation 1:7
[17] Michael H. Brown, *The Final Hour,* Queenship Publishing, Goleta, CA, 1992, page xii.

It would be something, wouldn't it? A report that Jesus was appearing in some remote place — just as Mary is appearing. We can only imagine the effect that would have. We can only imagine the flood of pilgrims.

Already we know what happened when the Blessed Mother appeared at Fatima, Lourdes and Medjugorje. Thousands and then millions — tens of millions, at each of those places — rushed to feel the grace associated with what theologians classify as first-tier "corporeal" apparitions.

They were not simple visions. They were not fleeting manifestations. They were first-tier apparitions — and how much more grace would there be if there was to be a first-class corporeal apparition of Jesus?

Such has never occurred, not since the Ascension. Yes, there have been many countless visions of the Lord, and He has been seen, allegedly, by countless individual mystics. [18]

Brown made his point clear. While Marian apparitions have been common and widespread, not a single "first-class corporeal" apparition of Christ can be documented. As Brown summarized:

No, He has been in the background, waiting for a much larger manifestation. It is like she has been preparing the way. It is like her appearances are a forerunner of how He will one day appear. At the same time we have to be cautious: if there is such an apparition, might it be a deception? Might it be what Scripture warns us about when it says not to

---

[18] www.spiritdaily.com/manifestation2.htm.

heed those who say Christ is appearing here or there or in the desert? [19]

Manifestations of "Christ"

While Michael H. Brown is obviously aware of the Scriptures found in the twenty-fourth chapter of Matthew warning about false appearances of Christ in relation to the Second Coming, it appears he does not take these warnings very seriously. On the same day, he posted a second article titled "Predictions Provoke Key Question: Do We Face Second Coming or a Manifestation?" In this article Brown provides an interesting scenario for the Second Coming that clearly points to the Eucharistic Christ:

> What might be meant by a "manifestation"? We're prompted to pose those questions due to the flurry of prophecies during the past twenty years and recent predictions that Jesus will soon manifest or even formally return. In our minds the key question: Which is likeliest—a manifestation or His actual Second Coming?...Will there be a multiplication of His alleged apparitions? Will there be an enhanced power (as well as miracles) associated with the Blessed Sacrament? [20]

Brown goes on to answer his own question, clarifying how he believes "Jesus" might appear here on planet earth in the future. While up until now, Marian apparitions have been commonplace, he suggests that similar kinds of appearances of Christ could happen in the future. He writes:

> Right now such manifestations are mainly associated with the Blessed Mother. Will they soon be

---

[19] Ibid.
[20] Michael H. Brown, http://spiritdaily.com/manifestation.htm, cited July 1, 2003.

predominately associated with Christ Himself? Will the day come when an image of Christ will miraculously appear (in the same way as the famed image of Guadalupe) or will He appear in the same way that Mary has appeared at places such as Lourdes, Medjugorje, and Fatima—*in apparition*? [21]

According to Brown, manifestations of this "apparitional Jesus" would have a tremendous impact on the world and the world's religions. Further, he suggests that a Catholic "seer" by the name of Maria Esperanza has predicted that Jesus will come in a form that many do not expect:

Might *this* be what will happen? Will Christ soon appear to people in various parts of the world as He did for those forty days following His Resurrection? We wonder because already there are reports of Muslims receiving dreams of Jesus, and at another Church-approved site, in Venezuela, at Betania (which means *Bethany*), seer Maria Esperanza has recently predicted that Jesus will come in a way that is "very different" than many conceive. [22]

Then Brown makes another key point. He clarifies that this "manifestation theory" fits the Catholic position on the Second Coming. This Roman Catholic view rejects the belief held by many Evangelical Christians that Christ will literally return and rule here on earth for one thousand years. Brown writes:

This reminds us of the biblical admonition that He will come as a "thief in the night" — and again hints, perhaps, more at a series of supernatural

---

[21] Ibid.
[22] Ibid.

manifestations than the Final Coming—contrary to many evangelical beliefs that He will come as an actual flesh-and-blood messiah to literally rule the earth for a thousand years. That conception is rejected by the Catholic Church. [23]

Though the literal reign of Christ for 1000 years on earth is rejected by the Catholic Church, the 20th chapter of the Book of Revelation is very clear. The literal millennial reign of Jesus is clearly described in this chapter: "And they [believers] lived and reigned with Christ for a thousand years" (Revelation 20:4).

Eucharistic Manifestations

Sadly, Brown and many others look more to apparitional messages than the Word of Truth. Michael Brown confirms that his manifestation theory is based on apparitional messages. The "Mary" who often calls herself the Mother of the Eucharist, predicts she will herald the coming reign of her son, the Eucharistic Christ. As Brown states:

> At Medjugorje the Madonna allegedly told seers on January 8, 1984: "*Do not think that Jesus is going to manifest Himself again in the manger; friends, He is born in your hearts.*" Does this hint at a Eucharistic manifestation, a spiritual renewal, which is also prophesied (as beginning shortly) by Maria Esperanza? "The same way He resurrected—that is how God is going to appear to you, to me, in that way, as an apparition," asserts the famous mystic, although we are left to discern if this is a formal coming or, again, a manifestation. [24]

---

[23] Ibid.
[24] Ibid.

The scenario that Michael Brown proposes regarding the Second Coming of Jesus is not unique. Over the past several years I have discovered there are many others who advocate a similar scenario.

In an article found on the perpetualadoration.org web site, we read that:

> Fr. Joseph Iannuzzi, OSJ agrees that Christ will reign gloriously on earth, not physically, but in the Eucharist. In his book *The Triumph of God's Kingdom in the Millennium and End Times: A Proper Belief from the Truth in Scripture and Church Teachings*, he argues from the writings of the Fathers and Doctors of the Church, from the Magisterium, and from Sacred Scripture that there will be a flowering of Christ's kingdom on earth which will last for a period of time, not necessarily a literal thousand years, during which Christ will reign gloriously on earth, not physically, but in the Eucharist. During this period he says that the Eucharistic Heart of Jesus will "cultivate in the faithful a spirit of intense adoration and worship never before seen." Perhaps the spread of perpetual adoration we are seeing is a sign of more to come! [25]

The World's Greatest Secret Revealed

Thomas W. Petrisko has written a book titled "Mother of the Secret: From Eucharistic Miracles to Marian Apparitions Heaven Has Sought to Illuminate and Defend What Was Once the Church's Greatest Secret." [26] Petrisko's book

---

[25] Online posting: www.perpetualadoration.org/ws2000.htm, cited April 28, 2004.
[26] Thomas W. Petrisko, "Mother of the Secret: From Eucharistic Miracles to Marian Apparitions Heaven Has Sought to Illumi-

explains what is meant by the Eucharistic Reign of Jesus. While Petrisko maintains the Presence of Christ in the Eucharist has always been a sacred belief of the Roman Catholic Church, the time is soon coming, he believes, when the entire world will witness Christ's Eucharistic reign.

As an overview, we can examine a statement made on the back cover of Petrisko's book:

> In *Mother of the Secret,* Dr. Thomas W. Petrisko traces for us the exciting history of this important part of our faith. And he reveals how what was once the Church's greatest secret is about to become the cornerstone of a glorious new era, an era in which Jesus Christ will soon come to reign throughout the world in the sacrament of the Holy Eucharist. [27]

Further, to clarify what Petrisko means by the "glorious new era in which Jesus Christ will come to reign throughout the world in the sacrament of the Holy Eucharist," he states:

> Visionaries foretell that mankind will move from a secular agnostic, practically atheistic realm into a world that basks in the reality of God and belief in the presence of the supernatural. The prophets say that mankind will then thrive on secure faith and confidence in this reality, for true peace will rule and the Church will reign supreme. Most notably, many Catholic visionaries insist that the world will at last come to deeply understand the power, the mercy and the grace that is available in the mi-

nate and Defend What Was Once the Church's Greatest Secret," Queenship Publishing Company, Santa Barbara, 1997.
[27] Ibid., back cover.

raculous True Presence of Jesus Christ in the Sacrament of the Holy Eucharist. [28]

Petrisko, like Michael Brown, agrees that "Mary" the mother of Jesus, will play a crucial role in the conversion process that must occur if the world is going to embrace the Eucharistic Reign of Christ. This apparitional woman has been announcing that there is a "new era" ahead in which the Eucharistic Christ will bring peace to the world. Petrisko states:

> According to the Virgin Mary, it is particularly the faith in this Eucharistic nourishment which will effect the greatest changes in this new era. Mary says that much of the world will not only come to believe this mystery, but also will partake in it. Indeed, it is said that the Triumph of the Immaculate Heart of Mary during our times will gloriously lead the world into a new era of true peace. At that time, the Holy Eucharist will be better known, appreciated and treasured. It will be a reign not just within the Church and individual lives, but in whole nations. Thus, the infinite power and grace available in the Eucharist will no longer be the world's greatest secret! [29]

The New Era

Given Petrisko's preceding scenario, it is clear that he believes the Eucharistic Christ along with the "Mother of the Eucharist" will soon play a major role in evangelizing the world to the Roman Catholic Church. Petrisko summarizes his vision of the future by quoting a statement made by Father Martin Lucia in an article written for the journal *Immaculata*:

---

[28] Ibid., page xii.
[29] Ibid., page xxiv.

The message of all the Marian apparitions, both past and present, is that the triumph of the Immaculate Heart of Mary will culminate in the Eucharistic reign of the Sacred Heat of Jesus. The Eucharistic reign will come through perpetual adoration of Jesus in the Blessed Sacrament. [30]

There are numerous others who support the idea that the Mother of the Eucharist and the Eucharistic Christ will soon manifest and rule and reign over the entire world. Ted and Maureen Flynn are the authors of *The Thunder of Justice,* [31] which investigates the prophetic side of messages coming from the Queen of Heaven. In their book, they state:

As John the Baptist prepared the way for the first coming of Jesus. Mary prepares the way for His Second Coming. Mary proclaims that a new world and era is upon us, and the triumph of Her Immaculate Heart and the Second Pentecost (the outpouring of the Holy Spirit) will usher in the Reign of the Sacred Heart of Jesus. The Blessed Mother spoke through Father Gobbi on October 13, 1990 about the glorious reign of Jesus and His Second Coming: "The glorious reign of Christ, which will be established in your midst and the Second Coming of Jesus into the world is close at hand. This is His return in glory. This is His glorious return, to establish His reign in your midst and to bring all humanity, redeemed by His Most Precious Blood, back to the state of His new terrestrial paradise. **That which is being prepared is so great that its**

---

[30] Ibid., page 268.
[31] Ted and Maureen Flynn, *The Thunder of Justice,* MaxKol Communications, Inc., Herndon, VA, 1993.

equal has never existed since the creation of the world." [32]

Global Reign

Is the last sentence of the above quote simply the dream of a few fringe Catholics? Consider the following. Father Don Stefano Gobbi is the head of the Marian Movement of Priests. Over 100,000 of the world's 400,000 Catholic priests are members of this organization. The Marian Movement of Priests have compiled a book containing hundreds of messages reportedly given to Father Gobbi from "Mary". Here is one example:

> Because in the Eucharist, Jesus Christ is really present, He remains ever with you, and this presence of His will become increasingly stronger, will shine over the whole earth like a sun and will mark the beginning of a New Era. The coming of the glorious reign of Christ will coincide with the greatest splendor of the Eucharist. Christ will restore His glorious reign in the universal triumph of His Eucharistic reign, which will unfold in all its power and will have the capacity to change hearts, souls, individuals, families, societies and the very structure of the world. [33]

As we have documented in chapter 4, the Catholic Eucharist is not the Jesus of the Bible. However, these authors, visionaries, and the pope himself, seem to place more weight on apparitions, experiences, and Church traditions, than they do on the Word of God. When we ignore

---

[32] Ibid., page 12, emphasis in the original.
[33] Fr. Don Stefano Gobbi, *To the Priests, Our Lady's Beloved Sons*, St. Francis, ME, The National Headquarters of the Marian Movement of Priests in the United States of America, 1998, page 528. Message given on August 21, 1987 to Father Gobbi.

God's warnings and accept extra-biblical revelations without testing them by the Bible, we are vulnerable to all manner of deception.

Bud MacFarlane Jr. is the author of the best-selling Catholic novel *Pierced By A Sword*. In this book, Mr. MacFarlane paints an amazingly detailed picture of end-time events, based not on the Bible, but mainly on apparitions, visionaries, and Church dogmas. Below is an excerpt:

> Within one year, on a Thursday, in the mountain village of Garabandal, Spain, a giant cross appeared in the sky above the pines. It was the Great Miracle of Garabandal. Millions present were instantly healed of mental and physical infirmities, as prophesied. The Cross was two stories tall, surrounded by an illuminated cloud, and was suspended thirty feet in the air above a patch of pine trees. Satellite television beamed its image around the world. People could walk up to it, look at it, but could feel nothing when they reached out to touch it.
>
> It was similar to the Cross that every person on the face of the earth had seen during the Great Warning. There was one difference: there was no corpus on the Garabandal Cross. **Suspended above it was a Sacred Host**. Streams of heavenly red and white light came forth from the Host. The Body of the Risen Christ. The misty cloud illuminated the Cross and Sacred Host at night.
>
> The Cross remains there to this day. Over two billion pilgrims came from all over the world to see it in person....**In addition, everyone "met" the Im-**

maculate Conception, Mary, at the foot of the Cross during their Warnings. [34]

Similar scenarios are given by scores of apparitions and believed on by millions of followers. Many additional sources could be quoted showing how professing Christians are being misled by apparitional messages, unreliable experiences, and unbiblical teachings.

What Does the Future Hold?

As previously stated in this chapter, the Bible teaches that Jesus is the Son of God. Jesus died on the cross, was resurrected from the dead, and then ascended into heaven to prepare a place for all those who will place their trust in Him alone. While He presently dwells in heaven, He will return. In the Book of Acts we are given details concerning Jesus' bodily ascension from the Mount of Olives into heaven. As Luke recorded:

> Now when He had spoken these things, while they watched, He was taken up, and a cloud received Him out of their sight. And while they looked steadfastly toward heaven as He went up, behold, two men stood by them in white apparel, who also said, "Men of Galilee, why do you stand gazing up into heaven? This *same* Jesus, who was taken up from you into heaven, will so come in like manner as you saw Him go into heaven." [35]

Note the clarity of the words that are used. This "same Jesus" who departed planet earth for heaven, "will so come in like manner as you saw Him go into heaven." Is there any way the Second Coming of Christ could be con-

---

[34] Bud MacFarlane, Jr., *Pierced By A Sword*, Fairview Park, OH, Saint Jude Media, 1995, pages 552, 553, [emphasis added].
[35] Acts 1:9-11

fused with future "manifestations" of a false christ appearing in churches worldwide?

Jesus Himself stated exactly how He would return. His return at the Second Coming will be seen by all. In Matthew 24 we read:

> Then the sign of the Son of Man will appear in heaven, and then all the tribes of the earth will mourn, and they will see the Son of Man coming on the clouds of heaven with power and great glory. [36]

The apostle John reiterated this truth in the Book of Revelation: "Behold, He is coming with clouds, and every eye will see Him, even they who pierced Him. And all the tribes of the earth will mourn because of Him. Even so, Amen." [37]

Notice that every person alive on the planet will witness the glorious appearance and return of Jesus Christ to earth. There is no possible way such a majestic appearance of Jesus Christ at the Second Coming could ever be compared to the so-called appearances of the Eucharistic Christ we are being told will someday transform the world.

Warning of Deception

Only those who rely on apparitions or private revelations or signs and wonders, could be deceived by Eucharistic manifestations. Only those who do not love and know God's Word, the Word of Truth, [38] could be per-

---

[36] Matthew 24:30
[37] Revelation 1:7
[38] Psalm 119:43; 2 Corinthians 6:7; Ephesians 1:13; 2 Timothy 2:15; James 1:18

suaded to believe that Eucharistic manifestations were equivalent to, or would precede His Second Coming.

> The coming of the lawless one is according to the working of Satan, **with all power, signs, and lying wonders, and with all unrighteous deception** among those who perish, **because they did not receive the love of the truth**, that they might be saved. And for this reason God will send them strong delusion, that they should believe the lie, that they all may be condemned who did not believe the truth but had pleasure in unrighteousness. [39]

In our concluding chapter we will explain our hope and the reason for writing this book—that you may receive eternal life in Jesus Christ by obeying the true gospel and following the only true God.

> And this is eternal life, that they may know You, the only true God, and Jesus Christ whom You have sent. [40]

---

[39] 2 Thessalonians 2:9-12
[40] John 17:3

Chapter Twelve
The Biblical Gospel and the Biblical Jesus

Time will tell whether or not the Eucharistic Jesus will reign in the world. However, the immediate question you must ask is—"Will the Eucharistic Jesus reign in my heart?" Will you trust "another" Jesus because of Rome or because apparitions endorse him? Will you trust "another" Jesus because you have experienced a miracle or felt a presence? Or will you follow the Jesus of the Bible?

Only the Bible, the Word of God, is infallible. [1] It is truth. [2] We know this by its fulfilled prophecies. There are dozens of prophecies concerning Christ alone that were fulfilled. In addition, there are hundreds of prophecies concerning Israel and the Gentile nations that have come to pass. The probability of all this happening by chance is too small to consider.

At least forty men in different countries, at different times, in three different languages, over a period of 1600 years penned the Sacred Word. They had no way of collaborating, yet the Bible has a unified theme. It tells one

---

[1] 2 Peter 1:20-21
[2] John 17:17

consistent story. No other book can boast of such intelligent design.

The Holy Bible has endured centuries of efforts to burn and banish it. Yet, as Jesus predicted it has survived. [3] In fact it has flourished. Today the Bible is available in over 2300 languages and dialects. [4] This amazing book records the life of the only perfect Person. No other book and no other man can compare.

There is no risk in accepting the Bible as our final authority.

Faith is not a Feeling

The Bible states simply, "We walk by faith, not by sight." [5] The Bible further explains that saving faith in God comes as we hear and obey the Word of God—"faith comes by hearing, and hearing by the word of God." [6] Christians are to follow Jesus Christ alone—who is the very word of God. [7] We must abide in Him. As the Bible states:

> If you abide in My word, you are My disciples indeed. [8]

> How can a young man cleanse his way? By taking heed according to Your word. [9]

---

[3] Matthew 24:35

[4] www.biblesociety.org. Portions or all of the Bible have been translated into over 2,300 languages and dialects covering over 90% of the world's population.

[5] 2 Corinthians 5:7

[6] Romans 10:17

[7] John 1:1, 14

[8] John 8:31

[9] Psalms 119:9

From childhood you have known the Holy Scriptures, which are able to make you wise for salvation through faith which is in Christ Jesus. [10]

However, the Bible cautions we are not to walk by sight (or appearances or visions or feelings or emotions). We all know that appearances can be misleading. Our senses can be deceived. Jesus warns us, "Do not judge according to appearance, but judge with righteous judgment." [11] During the last days seductive deceptions will multiply. Quoting from the Scriptures:

> The coming of the lawless one is according to the working of Satan, with all power, signs, and lying wonders. [12]

> But evil men and impostors will grow worse and worse, deceiving and being deceived. [13]

> Now the Spirit expressly says that in latter times some will depart from the faith, giving heed to deceiving (seducing) spirits and doctrines of demons. [14]

Feelings, Experiences, and Deceptions

A universal common denominator associated with the Eucharist and the apparitions involves reports of intense encounters and gratifying feelings. Many experience a sense of serenity. Others encounter a spiritual presence or warmth. Some see visions, while others commune with an apparition. However, as the previous Scriptures explain, Satan and his demons can conjure false signs, feelings, and

---

[10] 2 Timothy 3:15
[11] John 7:24
[12] 2 Thessalonians 2:9
[13] 2 Timothy 3:13
[14] 1 Timothy 4:1

experiences. These experiences can give the recipient a false sense of peace with God, while in reality they are leading the person into a trap.

While the Bible acknowledges that believers experience God in unique and often intense ways, it also warns that feelings, visions, emotions, and experiences can be of the deceptive sort. We are to seek the Lord in His Word. Any experience that occurs must be tested by God's Word. "Test all things; hold fast what is good." [15] If our spiritual filter is not God's law, His testimony, His word, we will be led astray:

> To the law and to the testimony! If they do not speak according to this word, it is because there is no light in them. [16]

Follow Your Heart or God's Law?

The world tells us to follow our heart—go with our feelings. The Bible, on the other hand, states emphatically—"He who trusts in his own heart is a fool, but whoever walks wisely will be delivered." [17] Our senses and feelings can direct us on a path that leads to destruction rather than life. We need a new heart—one guided by God and His trustworthy testimony. As the Bible states:

> There is a way that seems right to a man, But its end is the way of death. [18]

> The heart is deceitful above all things, and desperately wicked; who can know it? [19]

---

[15] 1 Thessalonians 5:21
[16] Isaiah 8:20
[17] Proverbs 28:26
[18] Proverbs 14:12
[19] Jeremiah 17:9

Cast away from you all the transgressions which you have committed, and get yourselves a new heart and a new spirit. [20]

God tells us we need new hearts. You may ask, "What's wrong with the heart I have?" Once again, it is God's Word that acts like a divine flashlight showing us the darkness and depravity of our old heart:

For the word of God is living and powerful, and sharper than any two-edged sword, piercing even to the division of soul and spirit, and of joints and marrow, and is a discerner of the thoughts and intents of the heart. [21]

For the commandment is a lamp, and the law a light. [22]

The Bad News

God tells us that we need new hearts. But how do we receive this new heart? Before explaining God's gracious provision, we must first understand mankind's dilemma. The Bible states that "all have sinned and fall short of the glory of God." [23] Scripture is emphatic—"They have all turned aside, they have together become corrupt; There is none who does good, no, not one." [24] This is why we cannot trust our old hearts. Our hearts are inclined to error and sin.

To see if God's assessment is fair and accurate, we need to look at His Ten Commandments (Exodus 20).

---

[20] Ezekiel 18:31
[21] Hebrews 4:12
[22] Proverbs 6:23
[23] Romans 3:23
[24] Psalm 14:3

Have you ever used your Creator's name (Jesus Christ or God) in vain, or worse, as a curse word? Think of how offensive this is to your Creator. This is the God who wove you in your mother's womb. He blessed you with eyes that behold His beautiful creation and taste buds that delight in His great variety of foods. Think of the wonder of your ears, and how music can inspire and refresh you. The truth is, "Every good gift and every perfect gift is from above, and comes down from the Father of lights." [25] Do you see why God considers blasphemy very serious?

Have you ever lied? White lies and fibs are lies in God's eyes. We're commanded to tell the truth, the whole truth, and nothing but the truth. Have you?

Have you ever stolen anything—the value is irrelevant? Cheating on a test or fudging the tax numbers is stealing. Please remember God sees the past as the present. He does not forget.

Have you ever committed adultery? Or have you secretly desired to? Jesus said, "But I say to you that whoever looks at a woman to lust for her has already committed adultery with her in his heart." [26]

Have you ever committed murder? Most plead innocent until they realize that hatred in the heart is murder in God's eyes: "Whoever hates his brother is a murderer, and you know that no murderer has eternal life abiding in him." [27] Think of the people you would like to get out of the way. Reflect on the many people who annoy you and those who caused you pain or embarrassment. To hate them in your heart is murder.

---

[25] James 1:17
[26] Matthew 5:28
[27] 1 John 3:15

If you answered "yes" to these questions, then by your own admission you are a blasphemer, a liar, a thief, an adulterer and a murderer at heart. When we sin, we sin against our Holy Creator. And God warns us that: "The wages of sin is death" (Romans 6:23). Sin causes both physical death and eternal death in the lake of fire. [28]

The Good News

Fortunately this is not the end of the story. The Good News is that "[God] is not willing that any should perish but that all should come to repentance" (2 Peter 3:9). In His great love, God became a man, in the person of Jesus Christ, to fulfill the law and to pay the penalty which our sins demanded. We sinned, yet Jesus died in our place. The Bible declares:

> God demonstrates His own love toward us, in that while we were still sinners, Christ died for us. [29]

> The wages of sin is death, but the gift of God is eternal life in Christ Jesus our Lord. [30]

> For God so loved the world that He gave His only begotten Son, that whoever believes in Him should not perish but have everlasting life. [31]

Jesus died in our place. He then rose from the dead defeating death. All who will turn (repent) from their sins and place their trust in Him will be saved. This is how we receive a new heart — and eternal life. This is what Jesus meant when He said we must be born again. [32] Our spirit

---

[28] Revelation 20:15
[29] Roman 5:8
[30] Romans 6:23
[31] John 3:16
[32] John 3:3, 7

is made alive when we simply believe in the Lord and His provision.

The Free Gift

It is important to understand that God offers salvation to all as a free gift. Only Jesus could pay the penalty that our sins demanded. We cannot bribe God with our "good works" or church attendance. No ritual or sacrament can appease His divine justice. We must rest fully on the merits of Jesus Christ. The Bible states:

> For by grace you have been saved through faith, and that not of yourselves; it is the gift of God, not of works, lest anyone should boast. [33]

> Knowing that a man is not justified by the works of the law but by faith in Jesus Christ. [34]

> Then they said to Him, "What shall we do, that we may work the works of God?" Jesus answered and said to them, "This is the work of God, that you believe in Him whom He sent." [35]

The Biblical Jesus

The Roman Catholic Jesus is the Eucharistic Jesus. The Marian apparition's Jesus is also the Eucharistic Jesus. However, the Eucharistic Jesus is not found in the Bible.

John chapter 1 states that Jesus is the Creator of all things. [36] He is eternal. [37] He is sinless. [38] He is immuta-

---

[33] Ephesians 2:8-9
[34] Galatians 2:16
[35] John 6:28-29
[36] John 1:1-3
[37] Revelation 1:8
[38] 1 John 3:5

ble—unchanging. [39] In Colossians chapter 1, we read that Jesus, the One who made everything, is the One who redeemed us from our sins. [40] The Word of God also states that Jesus is omnipotent, [41] omnipresent, [42] and omniscient. [43]

Isn't it reasonable to ask: how could Jesus, the eternal Creator, be dependent on a Roman Catholic priest to manifest His presence? Nowhere in the Bible does it state that Jesus can be placed and confined in a container made with human hands. Nor is a priest needed to invoke His presence.

Further, the fact that the Eucharistic Jesus is supposedly re-sacrificed at each Mass, demonstrates another major conflict with the Bible. In the Book of Hebrews we read:

> But Christ came as High Priest of the good things to come, with the greater and more perfect tabernacle not made with hands, that is, not of this creation. Not with the blood of goats and calves, but with His own blood He entered the Most Holy Place once for all, having obtained eternal redemption. For if the blood of bulls and goats and the ashes of a heifer, sprinkling the unclean, sanctifies for the purifying of the flesh, how much more shall the blood of Christ, who through the eternal Spirit offered Himself without spot to God, cleanse your conscience from dead works to serve the living God? And for this reason He is the Mediator of the new covenant, by means of death, for the redemption of the transgressions under the first covenant,

---

[39] Hebrews 13:8
[40] Colossians 1:13-18
[41] Philippians 3:21
[42] Matthew 28:20
[43] John 16:30

that those who are called may receive the promise of the eternal inheritance. [44]

According to Scripture, the ultimate sacrifice has been made "once for all". Jesus has "obtained eternal redemption". "It is finished," [45] as Jesus said. The upper room is vacated. The cross is bare. And the tomb is empty. Jesus has been resurrected. Halleluiah! He now dwells in the hearts of those who have trusted and believed on Him. Truly, this is reason for rejoicing!

Jesus said, "I am with you always, even to the end of the age" (Matthew 28:20). The apostle Paul tells us that Christ dwells in every believer's heart. [46] Christians are the temple of God — the Spirit of God dwells in us. [47] If ingesting the consecrated bread were the true way to receive Christ, it would only bring His presence for a short time. Only while the bread remained in the digestive tract would Christ be in you. The rest of the time He would be absent. Yet, the biblical Jesus told us, "Abide in Me, and I in you." [48] Jesus is always with every believer.

Serious Consequences

The Book of Hebrews appears to include a warning to those who crucify Christ repeatedly and put Him to an open shame. In the sixth chapter we read:

> Therefore, leaving the discussion of the elementary principles of Christ, let us go on to perfection, not laying again the foundation of repentance from dead works and of faith toward God, of the doc-

---

[44] Hebrews 9:11-15
[45] John 19:30
[46] Ephesians 3:17
[47] 1 Corinthians 3:16
[48] John 15:4

trine of baptisms, of laying on of hands, of resurrection of the dead, and of eternal judgment. And this we will do if God permits. For it is impossible for those who were once enlightened, and have tasted the heavenly gift, and have become partakers of the Holy Spirit, and have tasted the good word of God and the powers of the age to come, if they fall away, to renew them again to repentance, since they crucify again for themselves the Son of God, and put Him to an open shame. [49]

Are you willing to risk the chance of putting Jesus to an open shame by following the Eucharistic Christ? Keep in mind that Jesus was crucified once for sins. He shed His blood on the cross one time for all. The sacrifice has been made. Our sins have been paid in full.

Call Upon the True Jesus

If we will repent of (turn from and forsake) our sins and simply acknowledge what He has done and ask Him to forgive us for what we have done, then we can enter into a relationship with Jesus, our Creator and Redeemer, that will last forever. As Paul wrote to the Romans:

But what does it say? "The word is near you, in your mouth and in your heart" (that is, the word of faith which we preach): that if you confess with your mouth the Lord Jesus and believe in your heart that God has raised Him from the dead, you will be saved. For with the heart one believes unto righteousness, and with the mouth confession is made unto salvation. For the Scripture says, "Whoever believes on Him will not be put to shame." For there is no distinction between Jew and Greek, for the same Lord over all is rich to all who call upon

---

[49] Hebrews 6:1-6

Him. For "whoever calls on the name of the LORD shall be saved." [50]

Calling upon the Lord is all that is required. If we come before Him with a sincere heart and ask him to forgive us for our sins, He will.

In the Book of Acts, Luke recorded:

> Then Peter, filled with the Holy Spirit, said to them, "Rulers of the people and elders of Israel: If we this day are judged for a good deed done to a helpless man, by what means he has been made well, let it be known to you all, and to all the people of Israel, that by the name of Jesus Christ of Nazareth, whom you crucified, whom God raised from the dead, by Him this man stands here before you whole. This is the 'stone which was rejected by you builders, which has become the chief cornerstone.' Nor is there salvation in any other, for there is no other name under heaven given among men by which we must be saved." [51]

It is this Jesus, the Jesus of Nazareth, the "Jesus" Peter spoke about, who is the true Jesus. Let each one of us be sure that we know who He is because we know His word.

Prayer for Salvation

Dear Lord, Your Word says that if I will confess with my mouth the Lord Jesus and believe in my heart that He rose from the dead, I will be saved. For with the heart one believes unto righteousness, and with the mouth confession is made unto salvation.

---

[50] Romans 10:8-13
[51] Acts 4:8-12

I confess to You my sins and ask for Your forgiveness. I ask You to be my Lord and my Savior. Please guide and direct my life from this point on by Your Holy Spirit. Help me to know You better day by day as I read Your Word.

In the name of Jesus, Amen.

Appendix
Passion Evangelism

On Ash Wednesday 2004, *The Passion of the Christ* premiered in North America. Never has a film on Christ's passion garnered so much attention. In its first two weeks the movie grossed well over 200 million dollars and is poised to become the highest grossing R-rated movie in history. Its subsequent release around the world has the potential to influence multiplied millions of viewers.

Though *The Passion of the Christ* was produced and directed by a devout Roman Catholic — Mel Gibson, Catholics are not alone in the endorsement of this monumental movie. Perhaps the greatest support for the movie comes from Evangelical Bible-believing Christians. In an effort to win souls to Christ, these Christians are sponsoring all types of evangelistic events that revolve around the movie.

Among Christians, there is great excitement about the evangelistic potential of this film. Millions of souls, who would normally never discuss Jesus Christ, are now openly talking about this movie, and about Jesus — who He was and why He died.

However, as this appendix will explain, endorsing the movie without explaining the gospel can be dangerous. The first reason is quite clear: *The Passion of the Christ*, as the name indicates, focuses mainly on the passion (the sufferings) of Christ. The movie does not adequately explain the significance of these events. Many have died for noble causes, but Christ's death is unique. As Christians, we should springboard from discussions surrounding the movie to explain the full meaning and purpose of Christ's life, death, and resurrection.

Catholic Evangelism

Not surprisingly, many Catholics are also using the movie as an opportunity to evangelize. Ascension Press and Catholic Exchange have provided a Catholic guide and witnessing companion to the film entitled, *A Guide to the Passion: 100 Questions About "The Passion of the Christ."*

Author Matthew Pinto shared with Zenit news agency how the book will "help Catholics and non-Catholics understand the Eucharistic and Marian significance shown in the movie, know the case for Christ, learn about the Church Jesus instituted and respond accordingly in their faith lives." [1]

In the interview, Zenit asked author Matthew Pinto the following question—"Why is a particularly Catholic guidebook important in order to understand the movie?" Pinto replied:

A Catholic guide is necessary because the Gospels are completely Catholic, as is the movie. Even still, many will not see or understand the more sublime teachings that the director and writers are putting forth through this epic film.

---

[1] "A Guide to 'The Passion of the Christ,' Matthew Pinto on a Resource to Explain the Movie and Its Message," www.ewtn.com/WorldOver, cited February 23, 2004, (www.zenit.org).

A secular viewer, for instance, will probably not understand that the image of the serpent's head being crushed is a reference to Genesis 3:15. Likewise, the heavily Eucharistic and Marian emphasis of the film is something that a well-catechized Catholic will easily see, but many uncatechized Catholics and many Protestants will not deeply grasp.

As stated in the introduction to the book, understanding the profound Marian and Eucharistic imagery and theology really requires a deep understanding of Catholicism.

Our Protestant brothers and sisters, who are to be commended for their evangelical fervor and creativity in promoting this film, are generally not schooled in these issues. [2]

Further, Matthew Pinto explained that this "witnessing tool" would provide a "scene-by-scene commentary on the theological and artistic aspects of the film" to help Catholics educate and evangelize non-Catholics. When asked "Does the guide anticipate Protestant skepticism about the Eucharistic elements?" he replied:

We simply explain the connection between the sacrifice of Calvary and the sacrifice of the Mass.

The director uses a crosscutting technique in the movie that draws a parallel between the Last Supper and the crucifixion, and we explore this connection in the book. [3]

---

[2] Ibid.
[3] Ibid.

The interview finished with this question—"What response have you gotten from [Catholic] parishes and the faithful?" Pinto concluded with these words:

> We were confident that the response would be strong, but it has been far stronger than we expected. People love it. Someone proposed to me that this book is likely the fastest selling book in Catholic history—with advance sales of nearly 140,000 in two weeks—thanks to the power of the Internet and the timeliness of the book in relation to this major Catholic cultural event.

> I believe that the film presents one of the greatest watershed evangelization opportunities of our generation. [4]

The Goal and Effect of *The Passion of the Christ*

Some have asked the question: Was it Mel Gibson's intention for the film to focus on the Catholic Eucharist and Mary? In an interview given on EWTN, while explaining the "very moving and emotional and efficacious" aspects of the Catholic Latin Mass, Mr. Gibson stated his goal and intention for making this film:

> The goal of the movie is to shake modern audiences by brashly juxtaposing the "sacrifice of the cross with the sacrifice of the altar—which is the same thing." [5]

This interview was broadcast around the globe on EWTN—the world's largest Catholic television broadcasting organization. Of course, all Catholics are required by Rome to believe that Christ is repeatedly sacrificed on

---

[4] Ibid.
[5] http://tmatt.gospelcom.net/column/2004-01/21.

Catholic altars at every Mass. Might this movie influence others to embrace this unbiblical belief?

Though the lasting affects of this movie will not be known for some time, it has already had a profound influence on the cast and crew. Jim Cavaziel—the actor who played Jesus, explained how those involved in the film were changed. In the following statement made by Carl Limbacher taken from an article titled "Mel Gibson's 'Christ' Reveals Crucifixion," written January 25, 2004, we are told that many in the crew converted to Catholicism:

> In his first media interview anywhere about his starring role in Mel Gibson's much anticipated film "The Passion of the Christ," James Cavaziel—Gibson's Jesus—detailed on Friday the ordeal of filming the Crucifixion scenes, noting that the overall experience prompted many in the crew to convert to Catholicism. [6]

Further, Cavaziel stated that the filming of Christ's story "really changed people's lives." [7] According to the interview, Cavaziel also told Gibson, "I think it's very important that we have Mass every day—at least I need that to play this guy." [8]

Then one further statement that focuses in on the heart of the issue. Cavaziel said: "I felt if I was going to play him I needed the sacrament in me. Gibson provided that." [9]

Of course, the "sacrament" Cavaziel was referring to, is the Sacrament of the Eucharist. This is the heart and core of the Roman Catholic faith. As we have shown in chapter

---

[6] Carl Limbacher, NewsMax.com,
http://newsmax.com/archives/ic/2004/1/25/145119.shtml.
[7] Ibid.
[8] Ibid.
[9] Ibid.

4 of this book, the Eucharistic Christ is not the biblical Christ. We also know that having "the sacrament in me" is of no spiritual value. Do these men understand the biblical gospel?

The "Mary" Connection

In an article written by Catherine L. Keefe called "Journey of an Actor's Soul," Jim Caviezel shared how "Mary" prepared him to play this momentous role. Keefe, writing about Caviezel's spiritual journey stated:

> [Jim's] faith has grown in fits and starts. Some of his spiritual awakenings revolve around the Blessed Mother, the Rosary, and Medjugorje, Bosnia, where many believe the Virgin Mary has been appearing since 1981. He visited the site in November 2000. [10]

The article explained what took place when Jim Caviezel prayed with Ivan Dragicevic, a visionary from Medjugorje who travels the world speaking about his encounters with "Mary." At first Caviezel was doubtful about Ivan and his visions. However his prayer with Dragicevic changed the actor's mind. Quoting from the article:

> "I said to Ivan, 'Hey, I'm here, is she in this room?'" Dragicevic assured him that Mary was there, so Caviezel prayed, saying, "I don't know if I can believe you're here, but if you are, go ahead and microwave me. Go ahead and do whatever you have to do to my soul." He felt a sudden, en-

---

[10] Catherine L. Keefe, Online posting: http://www.catholicdigest.org/stories/200202074a.html, cited March 20, 2004.

compassing peace. "It was one of the most beautiful days of my life," he says. [11]

Caviezel wears a gold medal of Our Lady of Medjugorje on a gold chain around his neck, one of three medals. He also has a cross-shaped scapular that declares: "I am a Catholic, please call a priest." The third depicts Pope John Paul II. [12]

One more statement from the actor who plays the role of Jesus Christ in Mel Gibson's *The Passion of the Christ* gives more insight into what Caviezel believes:

Caviezel grows animated as he explains how Mary brings him closer to her Son Jesus, whose presence in the Eucharist is so meaningful to him. The Eucharist, he explains, inspires him to turn away from sin. That, in turn, makes his prayer life more sincere. [13]

Finally, in another interview recorded by the official Medjugorje web site, Mr. Caviezel reiterates how "Mary" at Medjugorje prepared him to play the role of Jesus.

The catharsis for me to play this role was through Medjugorje, through Gospa. In preparation, I used all that Medjugorje taught me. Mel Gibson and I were going every day for Mass together. Some days I couldn't go for Mass, but I was receiving the Eucharist. [14]

---

[11] Ibid.
[12] Ibid.
[13] Ibid.
[14] http://www.medjugorje.org/mpb193.htm, cited March 10, 2004. Article also available at www.spiritdaily.com.

Cavaziel also has explained the role he believes the apparition of Mary played in bringing the film to life:

> This film is something I believe was made by Mary for her Son. Because it was made by her, it will be attacked by the enemy... [15]

The Catholic Mary

By searching the Scriptures, we know that the "Mary" of the apparitions is of demonic origin, and that the Eucharistic Jesus is a false christ. As Bible-believing Christians we must use every opportunity to explain who Jesus is and clarify the gospel of grace to those who are confused.

However, many Christians are apparently unaware that the producer of *The Passion* embraces a false christ and an unbiblical Mary. In fact, Mel Gibson endorses the Catholic notion that Mary is "a tremendous co-redemptrix and mediatrix." In an interview with *Christianity Today*, Mel told of his amazement that evangelical Christians were among the most receptive to his film depiction of Christ and Mary. Here are two excerpts from the interview:

> "I've been actually amazed at the way I would say the evangelical audience has—hands down—responded to this film more than any other Christian group." What makes it so amazing, he says, is that "the film is so Marian." [16]

> Gibson knows that Protestants don't regard Mary in the way Catholics do. And Gibson goes beyond many when he calls her "a tremendous co-redemptrix and mediatrix." [17]

---

[15] Ibid.

[16] http://www.christianitytoday.com/movies/commentaries/passion-melmarymothers.html, cited March 6, 2004.

[17] Ibid.

During *The Passion,* we see much of Jesus' agony through Mary's eyes. The strong spiritual link between Jesus and Mary is prominent throughout the movie. Her participation, her "co-redemptrix" work, is also suggested in the film. Yet, many Christians do not recognize the significance.

Two more quotes from the *Christianity Today* article show that the response to the Mary of the movie has been profound:

> Gibson says, "The way the film displays [Mary] has been kind of an eye opener for evangelicals who don't understand the reality of a mother and a son." [18]

> And that is what I observed: After both of *The Passion* screenings I attended, the Protestant women talked about identifying with Mary as a mother who was watching her child suffer. From whatever point in his spirituality Gibson's treatment of Mary is springing, it is touching deeply the maternal impulse in his viewers. [19]

Of course Mary did suffer during her Son's passion. [20] However, the biblical narrative does not focus on Mary. The focus of the Bible—from Genesis to Revelation—is the Father's great love for mankind. The eternal God and Creator demonstrated His great love for the world by sending His only begotten Son to die for our sins. While Jesus does call on the Father several times in the movie, Mary is given a much more prominent role than the Bible gives her. Where did Mel receive his inspiration to include these unbiblical scenes?

---

[18] Ibid.
[19] Ibid.
[20] Simeon's prophecy in Luke 2:35 anticipates this.

The Dolorous Passion of Our Lord Jesus Christ

Mr. Gibson has publicly stated that his film is based, in part, on visions and messages received by a nineteenth century Catholic mystic. The revelations and visions of Sister Anne Catherine Emmerich are contained in the book entitled — *The Dolorous Passion of Our Lord Jesus Christ*. The book states, "she was accustomed to have divine knowledge imparted to her in visions of all kinds, and was often favored by visits from the Mother of God and Queen of Heaven." [21]

The back cover of the book gives this description:

The *Dolorous Passion* recounts with incredible precision the horrendous sufferings undergone by our Savior in His superhumanly heroic act of Redemption. Also illuminating is its description of Mary's participation in the sufferings of her Son, so that this book gives the reader a poignant understanding of why Our Lady is often called our "Co-Redemptrix" and "Queen of Martyrs." [22]

The dedication page reads: "To the Immaculate Heart of the Virgin Mary, Mother of God, Queen of Heaven and Earth, Lady of the Most Holy Rosary, Help of Christians, and Refuge of the Human Race." [23]

Because of the tremendous interest in *The Passion of the Christ*, this book has become an instant best seller. Catholic bookstores rightly market it as "The Book That Inspired

---

[21] Anne Catherine Emmerich, *The Dolorous Passion of Our Lord Jesus Christ*, Tan Books and Publishers, Rockford, IL, 1983, page 3.
[22] Ibid., back cover.
[23] Ibid., dedication page.

Mel Gibson to Film *The Passion of the Christ.*" [24] The following quotes taken directly from Anne Catherine Emmerich's book, will confirm that Mel Gibson received much of his unbiblical Marian and Eucharistic scenes from this Catholic visionary:

> The Blessed Virgin was ever united to her Divine Son by interior spiritual communications; she was, therefore, fully aware of all that happened to him — she suffered with him, and joined in his continual prayer for his murderers. [25]

> I soon after saw Mary and Magdalen approach the pillar where Jesus had been scourged;...they knelt down on the ground near the pillar, and wiped up the sacred blood with the linen Claudia Procles [Pontius Pilate's wife] had sent. [26]

> [at the foot of the cross] the Blessed Virgin, filled with intense feelings of motherly love, entreated her Son to permit her to die with him... [27]

> She looked once more upon her beloved Son — ...the flesh of her flesh, the bone of her bone, the heart of her heart. [28]

There are many other unbiblical inclusions in the film that come straight from this book. For example, in the movie, after Peter denies Jesus, he falls at Mary's feet and says, "Mother, I have denied Him." (This episode is from page 174 of the book). The unbiblical character Veronica who wipes Jesus' bloody face is taken straight from the

---

[24] http://www.passion-movie.com/promote/book.html, cited March 12, 2002.
[25] Anne Catherine Emmerich, page 172.
[26] Ibid., pages 224-225.
[27] Ibid., page 283.
[28] Ibid., page 294.

book as well (pages 258-259). The manner that Mary receives and cradles Jesus (Pieta style) is also directly from this book (page 316).

The Eucharist in the Film and Book

Another major theme of *The Dolorous Passion* is its repeated references to the Eucharistic Jesus. In the book, as in the movie, Jesus refers to the "cup" as the "chalice" both in the Garden of Gethsemane and at the Last Supper. Catholics will understand this Eucharistic reference. Additionally, the Last Supper reenactment also comes straight from the book:

> Jesus was seated between Peter and John, the doors were closed, and everything was done in the most mysterious and imposing manner. When the chalice was taken out of its covering, Jesus prayed, and spoke to his Apostles with the utmost solemnity. I saw him giving them an explanation of the Supper, and the entire ceremony, and I was forcibly reminded of a priest teaching others to say Mass. [29]

The book is replete with references to the "Sacrifice of the Mass", the "Real Presence", and the "Blessed Eucharist". Not surprising, during the movie, when the bread is unwrapped, the camera flashes to a scene of Jesus being stripped. As Jesus' blood is dripping from the cross, the camera flashes to a scene where wine is being poured into a chalice during the Last Supper.

In the movie, when accusations are being hurled at Jesus at his trial, John 6 is quoted by an irate Jew saying that this man said we must "eat his body and drink his blood for eternal life." This scene is also straight from the book. [30]

---

[29] Ibid., page 83.
[30] Ibid., page 158.

Of course, this accusation is not recorded in the Bible, but the film's implication is clear — The stubborn false accusers deny transubstantiation, while those faithful to Jesus know this is the key to eternal life.

Here is one last excerpt from the book that concurs with Mel's Catholic beliefs:

> It was made known to me (Emmerich) that these [evil manifestations] were all those persons who in divers ways insult and outrage Jesus, really and truly present in the Holy Sacrament. I recognized among them all those who in any way profane the Blessed Eucharist. [31]

Lasting Effects

Understandably, many Christians are unaware of the Catholic references in the movie. The extra-biblical scenes are seen as simply artistic license or harmless Catholic affinities. However, this is clearly not the case.

Mel Gibson has stated that the movie "reflects my beliefs." [32] He also has said, "There is no salvation for those outside the [Catholic] Church...I believe it." [33] Though Mel has flip-flopped on this since, it is clear that Mel is a Catholic director with Catholic theological advisors, producing a Catholic movie, intended to evangelize people into the Catholic Church. According to the Catholic web site, Catholic Passion Outreach:

> The Passion of the Christ offers a once-in-a-lifetime opportunity for you to spread, strengthen, and

---

[31] Ibid., page 114.
[32] www.ewtn.com/WorldOver/, cited February 17, 2004.
[33] The New Yorker, September 15, 2003.

share the Catholic faith with your family and friends. [34]

Michael Brown, a Catholic author and provider of the web site *Spirit Daily*, has written and reported on *The Passion of the Christ* extensively on his web site. In his February 28, 2004 article entitled "Passion is seen as a movie with potential to cause profound and lasting effects," he explains the role the movie may have in uniting Christians.

> Granted, it's only a movie, but it could help unite Christians. I have never seen a better possibility for popular ecumenical dialogue. We all have common ground—and though Gibson is Catholic (a traditionalist at that), his most fervent support so far has come from   Baptists, Pentecostals, and Evangelicals. [35]

Besides the film's potential for uniting Christians and spurring ecumenical dialogue, Mr. Brown notes some other potential results of the movie:

> Another [effect] involves Mary. This movie presents the Blessed Mother in a way that reintroduces her to Protestants. They are able to see her as someone they can relate to. She is down to earth. They will laugh with her. They will cry with her. They'll more fully appreciate (as will everyone else) what *she* went through. Hopefully, they'll grow to love her.

---

[34] http://passion.catholicexchange.com/, cited March 11, 2004.
[35] http://www.spiritdaily.com/gibsonviewing.htm, cited February 28, 2004.

During the Last Supper scenes, they may also gain a better understanding of the Eucharist. [36]

Our Commission

There is no doubt that Mel Gibson is sincere. He and the multitudes of Catholics who have embraced the Catholic Mary and the Eucharistic Jesus are earnest in their desire to lead souls into the Catholic Church. However, though sincere, they are also deceived. Not all Catholics are aware of Rome's unbiblical teachings concerning Mary and the Eucharist. Nevertheless, many have embraced these deceptions. May we, as believers, heed Paul's final exhortation to Timothy:

> Preach the word! Be ready in season and out of season. Convince, rebuke, exhort, with all longsuffering and teaching. For the time will come when they will not endure sound doctrine, but according to their own desires, because they have itching ears, they will heap up for themselves teachers; and they will turn their ears away from the truth, and be turned aside to fables. But you be watchful in all things, endure afflictions, do the work of an evangelist, fulfill your ministry. [37]

As Christians, we must be equipped to present the truth in love. Often this requires that we expose deception with the light of God's Word.

Remember also that there is much good resulting from this controversy. Many Christians have been given a unique platform to give public testimony of why Jesus died and rose from the dead. Many other Christians are

---

[36] Ibid.
[37] 2 Timothy 4:2-5

using the movie as an opportunity to witness at theaters and other venues.

People are searching for spiritual meaning, purpose, and satisfaction. May the Lord enable each one of us by His Spirit to be faithful witnesses to this generation. May we testify of the Word of Truth [38] and point souls to the Word of Life — Jesus Christ. [39]

---

[38] Ephesians 1:13
[39] 1 John 1:1

Other Books on Related Topics

Biblical Insights for Contemporary Issues
by Roger Oakland

In *Biblical Insights for Contemporary Issues*, Roger Oakland equips Christians to think critically and analytically about the topics that confront them day to day. The book is a catalyst causing skeptics to rethink some of their deeply held though falsely assumed beliefs. In this easy-to-read, yet challenging book, Roger Oakland analyzes current trends that are affecting lives today and offers conclusions that are based upon truths found in the Word of God.

Available at www.understandthetimes.org
Or by calling 1-800-689-1888

New Wine and the Babylonian Vine
by Roger Oakland

In *New Wine and the Babylonian Vine*, Roger Oakland, documents the direction experience-based Christianity is heading and how it is joining together with experience-based Catholicism, other religions and a spiritualized environmentalism to form a global spirituality. Could this be the ecumenical delusion that the Bible predicts will unfold in the last days?

Available in book, two tape audio pack and video (two one-hour PowerPoint presentations).

Available at www.understandthetimes.org
or by calling 1-800-689-1888

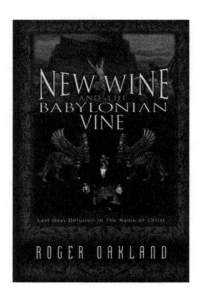

Messages From Heaven
by Jim Tetlow

Tens of millions of people visit apparition sites hoping to encounter the Blessed Virgin Mary. Those who follow the apparitions believe Mary has come back to turn us back to God, while others insist that these are either fabrications or the workings of Satan. Does the Bible anticipate apparitions, signs and wonders in the last days? Does the Word of God reveal the origins of these phenomena?

Available in book or video at www.understandthetimes.org or by calling 1-800-689-1888

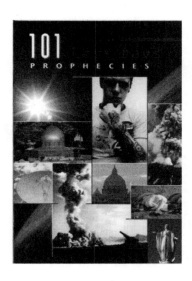

101 Last Days Bible Prophecies

The Bible predicts many specific signs that will culminate in the last days. This booklet highlights 101 prophecies that are coming to pass in our time, demonstrating that the Bible is indeed the inspired Word of God and that the end of all things is at hand.

Available at www.understandthetimes.org
or by calling 1-800-689-1888

Queen of All
by

Jim Tetlow, Roger Oakland and Brad Myers

According to the Book of Revelation, a woman will reign as queen over the kings of the earth in the last days. It is time to uncover the mystery and expose the identity of this "Queen." The Bible discloses that the activities surrounding the queen will affect the whole world. What can we do to prepare for what may soon take place? This book presents God's answer.

Available soon at www.understandthetimes.org
or by calling 1-800-689-1888